Couture to Chaos

National Gallery of Victoria

Couture to Chaos

Fashion from the 1960s to now

from the collection of the National Gallery of Victoria

Robyn Healy

Photography by Helen Skuse

Sponsored by

Supported by

Published by the National Gallery of Victoria

180 St Kilda Road, Melbourne, Victoria, 3004

National Library of Australia Cataloguing-in-Publication
entry:

National Gallery of Victoria.
Couture to chaos: fashion from the 1960s to now from
the collection of the National Gallery of Victoria.

Bibliography.
ISBN 0 7241 0188 8.

1. National Gallery of Victoria - Exhibitions. 2.
Costume - History - 20th century - Exhibitions. 3.
Costume design - History - 20th Century - Exhibitions.
4. Fashion - History - 20th century - Exhibitions. 5.
Fashion and art - Exhibitions. 6. Costume - Victoria -
Melbourne - Exhibitions. I. Healy, Robyn. II. Title.

391.0090450749451

Designer: Roger Saddington
Editor: Deidre Missingham
Word processor: Judy Shelverton
Film reproduction: Colorific Lithographics
Printer: Buscombe Printers
Photographer: Helen Skuse

Cover illustration:

Peter TULLY

Australia 1947–1992

Early flight attendant's vest 1990

lamé, metallic thread, retrospectra graphic plastic

Purchased from Admission Funds 1991   CT1-1991

Contents

Sponsor's Message

Myer is delighted to be continuing its support of the National Gallery of Victoria in presenting *Couture to chaos: fashion from the 1960s to now.*

Since the early 1990s, Myer has had a commitment to bringing the most exciting Australian and international fashion to the public and encouraging the development of fashion innovation in this country.

Couture to chaos is a very appropriate exhibition for the company to support at the National Gallery of Victoria and in our own Myer Melbourne store.

Terry McCartney
Managing Director

Acknowledgments

I would like to thank the staff of the National Gallery of Victoria for their various contributions: Kate Somerville (Curatorial Assistant Fashion and Textiles) for her endless support, ideas, enthusiasm and a lot of hard work; our Textile Conservator, Abigail Hart, who has conserved and prepared many of the works, often with unusual problems that are only associated with late 20th century materials; Helen Skuse (Photographic Services) for her beautiful photographs and Roger Saddington (Graphic Design) for the catalogue design and concept. Special thanks also to Daryl West-Moore (Chief Exhibitions Designer) and Fiona Wilson (Exhibitions Designer) for the exhibition layout. Thanks also to Judy Shelverton (Publications) for the manuscript preparation, Jennie Maloney (Publications) and editorial consultant Deidre Missingham. Warm thanks also to volunteers Genevive Tucker and Amanda Swanson for installation preparation.

Also thanks for the support of the following staff: Michael Watson (Chief Librarian), Shelley Marsh (Public Relations), Judy Williams and Judith Buckeridge (Business Council), Karen Quinlan (former Curatorial Assistant Fashion and Textiles), John McPhee (Deputy Director of Australian Art and Exhibitions Management), and Derek Gillman (Deputy Director International Art, Collection Management). This exhibition has only been made possibly by the generous support of our donors and lenders, in particular Georgina Weir and Janet Purves of Le Louvre, who helped us with information, donations and enthusiasm to develop our fashion collection to a world standard. Our other important contributors include the Women's Association of the National Gallery of Victoria, in particular the president Sandra Velik; Mary Lipshut, who has supported the collection since 1983 with garments and invaluable information; and Wendy Marshall of Elle Boutique, Perth, for her generous gift of Comme des Garçons garments.

Thank you to all our donors: Bernadette Anderton, Robyn Beeche, Rowena Clarke, Andrea Coote, Olivia Cuming, Rodney DeSoos, Patricia Forster, Melissa Janis, Anthony Knight, Rosalyn Marsh, Irene Mayes-Ryan, John McPhee, James Mollison AO, Uta Pearson, Gabrielle Pizzi, Jennifer Phipps, Mavis Powell, Rae Rothfield, Miss Sheila Scotter AM MBE, Cynthia Staley, Loti Smorgon, Ann Testro, Paul Trevillian and Robert Whitehead. Thanks also for advice and information from Christine Barro, Zambesi, Six, Iris Moar and Jenny Bannister; and to the librarians at the National Gallery of Australia, Margaret Shaw and Helen Hyland, for assistance in locating books and the use of their library. Special thanks to the previous Director of the National Gallery of Victoria, James Mollison AO, for his continuing interest and support.

Special thanks also to the sponsors, Myer, for their commitment beyond retail to support fashion in an art gallery.

Finally, thanks especially to our Director, Timothy Potts, for his excitement and support for this project over several years: this is much appreciated.

Director's Foreword

Couture to chaos: fashion from the 1960s to now represents a major breakthrough in the appreciation and documentation of recent fashion history in Australia. Representing the leading international and Australian designers, the exhibition is drawn principally from the collection of the National Gallery of Victoria, which we have been actively building over recent years to make this event possible. It takes the story of fashion design from the death of Christian Dior in 1957, forming a sequel to our very successful *Worth to Dior* exhibition of 1993. At the centre of the exhibition concept is its concern to represent costume in the context of a visual arts environment, thus acknowledging recent fashion artists and their clothing designs as the major forces in contemporary art that they have unquestionably become.

Couture to chaos addresses the interpretation of fashion within this broader arts environment and examines each decade from the 1960s until now, with an emphasis on key designers and major stylistic trends. In recent years, fashion has become increasingly diversified in approach and form. The exhibition and catalogue reflect this multiplicity by representing the various types of fashion artists and clothing forms at their very best and most adventurous.

The Gallery's collection of twentieth-century fashion has developed enormously in recent years through both gifts and acquisition. Our many generous donors have helped to fill a number of essential areas in the collection. It can be particularly difficult to obtain garments and accessories by contemporary designers, perhaps because we tend sometimes to undervalue the significance of works which were so recently items of regular use.

Special thanks go to our enthusiastic lenders to the exhibition, who have allowed our curator Robyn Healy into their wardrobes and given us the opportunity to display their garments in the context of our collection. Last year the Fashion and Textile department moved into a new storage and viewing area, allowing us much greater access and improved working conditions for dealing with large and often awkward pieces.

This is the third in a series of exhibitions and catalogues produced by the Gallery that focus on twentieth-century fashion, following *Balenciaga: Masterpieces of fashion design* in 1992 and *Worth to Dior: twentieth-century fashion design* in 1993. In the future we plan to showcase earlier periods from our collection, especially our remarkable Schofield collection of nineteenth-century costumes and our significant holdings of eighteenth- and nineteenth-century embroidery and lace.

I would particularly like to thank Myer as sponsor of *Couture to chaos* for their very generous support.

Timothy Potts
Director

Couture to Chaos

Interpretations of fashion — an introduction

LE LOUVRE, Melbourne est. c. 1927
Lillian Wightman, founder and chief designer
1903–1992
Evening bolero c. 1965
silk and metallic threads, glass beads,
plastic sequins
Presented through The Art Foundation of
Victoria by Janet Purves, Member 1995
1995.317

LE LOUVRE, Melbourne est. c. 1927
Lillian Wightman, founder and chief designer
1903–1992
Evening bolero c. 1965
silk, plastic sequins, glass beads
Presented through The Art Foundation of
Victoria by Georgina Weir, Member 1995
1995.321

Fashion is popular art, a responsive and interactive medium. It is an art form that combines aspects of decorative art and industrial design, a part of popular culture and social history. It is a symbolic system, a protective clothing form and even a kind of performance art.[1] All are areas worthy of serious contemplation and acknowledgement.

Fashion stimulates dialogue, as everyone always has an opinion about its aesthetic and relevance. Fashion is exhibited and collected by an art gallery in order to give the public an appreciation of the artist/designer's creative ideas and inspire ways for the viewer to understand the garment's fabrication, innovation and visual appeal. Exhibiting clothing as an art form is often challenged for inadequately realising the potential of costume, because it ignores the people who wore the garments, though not all interpreters need to dissociate fashion from the artist or creator. For a gallery ideally all garments purchased should be brand new, unworn, in mint condition. If otherwise, the wearer of the garment is usually unknown. In an art gallery it is legitimate to focus primarily on the clothing, its maker and/or designer in the context of the gallery's entire visual arts collection, in order to represent those artists who have chosen specifically to design and create garments.

Clothing is often taken for granted because it is worn by everyone. Frequently a concern with fashion is perceived as a frivolous pastime or a waste of time. But fashion is a powerful force and aesthetic, and an alluring area to study because of its pluralism and controversial nature.

Everyone is affected by fashion, even those who refuse to acknowledge this. It surrounds us every day and confronts us in a multitude of media and on the streets. Its symbols and signs relating to people and what they want to be are often stimulating and deliberately provocative.

Fashion cannot simply be judged for its wearability or by an expensive price tag. Like other forms of decorative arts it has a specific function. But it can also be perceived in terms of the fashion artist's use of original ideas, form, construction, and the subtleties of colour, texture, use of fabric, innovative materials and the juxtaposition of all these elements to produce a garment.

The creators of fashion and their varied approaches to clothing design can be studied like a branch of art history. Fashion can successfully both fuse and blur the distinctions between high and popular art. Costume represents the contemporary aesthetic of its day, developed by the designer and chosen to be worn by the wearer, as a means of expression and projection of self image. Major galleries all over the world have collections of costume that represent a social history of dress. A fashion collection that focuses on the major designers and makers working in this area is usually the province of art galleries.

The two leading costume curators at New York's Costume Institute at the Metropolitan Museum of Art, Richard Martin and Harold Koda, believe that: 'Scholarship and the museums have made peace with an expanded view of art and the partial congruity of fashion as a commercial art with other aesthetic forms.'[2] Yet have we?

The English feminist historian Elizabeth Wilson finds it 'Strange that when so much else has changed there exists such a strong hostility to fashion'. She goes on to explain that 'Fashions in clothing are, of course open to the objection that although we "need" clothes we don't "need" fashion'.[3] Colin McDowell, a serious scholar of fashion, notes with regret that the major cause of neglect and intelligent interest in this area is caused by 'Fear of Society, fear of oneself, fear of the power of clothing; fear is the reason fashion is so often dismissed as flippant and foolish'.[4] The author Nicholas Coleridge also points to the problem of the language of fashion contributing to this attitude, from magazines to the industry itself:

It uses language so indiscriminately that it has actually created a parallel vocabulary, in which everyday words take on specific fashion connotations, entirely misleading to the outside world ... 'Basic' (as in 'your basic wardrobe', 'your best basic') and essential ('the essential black leather skirt') are straightforward antitheses when hijacked by fashion writers.[5]

Words like 'now', 'fresh', 'in', 'out' and 'classics' are staples for categorisations and meaningless descriptions. Particular words also revolve around the nature of collections which are seasonal — 'autumn/winter', 'spring/summer' — and the purpose of the garment — eveningwear, daywear, after five — and even sexual demarcation categories, with menswear and womenswear. These terms are traditional and have evolved from buying and merchandising patterns.

Significantly, in 1982 the international art magazine *Artforum* published an Issey Miyake costume on its cover and acknowledged fashion in a broader artistic scheme. The issue produced what is possibly one of the most succinct definitions of fashion:

Fashion is a system of abstract signs which have no meaning beyond that determined by a maximum acceleration and proliferation of messages. In fashion the speed of communication is such that meaning disappears and changes from year to year, and lives only within the cyclical notion of the collections. The perpetual turnover of style resurrects previous models. If Modernism's vision of the future has been identified with hostility to the past, then fashion's continual reckless ingestation of the phantom of history could be what makes it a modern idea.[6]

VIVIENNE WESTWOOD, London est. 1971
Vivienne Westwood, designer
Great Britain born 1941
Platform shoe 1994
patent leather
Purchased 1994   CT431-1994

From a Postmodern perspective fashion should now be a respectable discipline to study and absorb. Its many sources and influences acknowledge its artistic nature as a significant part of our popular art and culture.

The important American costume collector and dealer Beverley Birks of New York notes that:

Only in the last twenty years has there been any real scholarship on costume ... Almost invariably, experts have approached the subject from the sociological standpoint. It's mostly how costume defined an era. Or fashion seen through the prism of feminism. Or the effect of elitism. Or the role of sportswear. Very few people simply talk about the clothes.[7]

When we study the artists of fashion, we are interested in how and why it was made and by whom, and in stylistic trends, fashion's visual effect then and now. We want to know more about the creative pool of the designer's ideas, including the application of new technology in certain materials and fastening mechanisms, about new ways of fabrication and technical details introduced for the attraction of the viewer. The use of new fabrics and dyes of certain colours — for instance, Courrèges' 'toxic' orange, or the use of new technology to make paper for dresses in the 1960s — can still startle us.

The distance time allows always seems to give garments some sort of credibility: what was once only a costume becomes something worthy of serious contemplation, usually after a respectful distance of fifty years. Contemporary work is easier to dismiss. 'People are embarrassed and rather afraid to take anything seriously to do with dress and appearance.'[8]

A confusing factor concerning fashion as art is that it works in multiples. This is its power and also can be perceived as a weakness. However, just because something is produced in quantity and is not unique, its significance is not necessarily lessened or weakened. Many of the garments on display are not couture garments or even very expensive, but rather, they are ready-to-wear clothes purchased from a boutique or department store. Innovation and creativity can override quality and practicality. Multiples are a feature of fashion; the more successful the design the more it is seen. It is the continuing desire for something new that eventually destroys the initial impact of a garment. Clothing that is popular should make us wonder how it achieved this success.

Clothes in their time and today reflect important design trends in fashion. For instance, prejudice in relation to natural versus synthetic fabrics or machine or handmade clothing is irrelevant without considering all elements of the garment. Designers often introduce a style or apply materials or constructions that are intended to shock and challenge traditional norms, and can be either accepted or rejected for this reason.

Exhibition mode

The nature of world fashion has changed radically since the 1960s. The exhibition *Couture to chaos*, drawn from the fashion collection of the National Gallery of Victoria, focuses on aspects of fashion design, and examines some of the new and stimulating directions that have occurred since 1960. On display from 11 September to 11 November 1996, the exhibition and this publication are designed as a sequel to the *Worth to Dior* exhibition, staged at the Gallery in 1993, which focused on the development of the fashion artist and the haute couture system of fashion.

Couture to chaos represents over thirty fashion designers with sixty costumes and accessories. It explores some of the major themes and fashion styles, such as the use of industrial materials, optical effects, recycled elements; the introduction of new forms of costume such as trousers and knee-high boots; and the influence of some of the street sub-culture groups on the work of fashion artists.

ANDREW McDONALD, Sydney est. 1994
Andrew McDonald, designer
Australia born 1962
Mule 1995
barramundi skin, suede, leather
Gift of Paul Trevillian 1995   1995.762-a-b

CHANEL
BOUTIQUE
40

This survey is not an encyclopaedic journey or a selection of all the top designers of this period, if one could ever be so bold or have the space to attempt this. Instead, it focuses on some important aspects of fashion design, examining the actual garment and the designer's artistic rationale. Varied approaches to clothing design are covered, from a selection of fashion systems for both male and female customers, and including designers from Australia. From the elite world of couture garments to the work of young local designers, no one direction or style predominates. Today no single designer can exert power over the direction of fashion. Fashion involves an enormous range of people other than the designer figure head, working at various levels. Our exhibition labels and captions recognise these people by always including the particulars of the fashion house or business.

Since the 1960s the dominance of couture fashion has waned; ready-to-wear clothing, the cult of youth, new synthetic materials and the changing needs of women have altered the role of fashion. No longer does the fashion world revolve solely around seasonal couture collections held in Paris, and dominated by a few designers. Fashion today is global and eclectic. Designers come from a range of backgrounds and take their inspiration from diverse sources — from the street, the past, the work of known great designers and cultures; and they have accepted advanced computer technology and the gradual breaking away from traditional making processes and materials.

There is both artistic and commercial pressure to continually make new forms of clothing. Designers have exploited the past and even revived fashions of recent decades, until style can no longer belong or be synonymous with a particular decade: 'we embrace the Postmodern — a style which looks back with affection rather than anger or superiority — dated styles are re-contextualised'.[9]

CHANEL, Paris est. 1914–39
re-opened 1954
Karl Lagerfeld, designer
Germany born 1939
Jenny Kee, textile designer
Australia born 1947
Label for *Suit* 1983
comprising jacket, blouse, skirt and necklace
silk, metal
Gift of the House of Chanel through
Vogue Australia 1983   CT105-1983

ISSEY MIYAKE, Tokyo est. 1971
Issey Miyake, designer
Japan born 1935
Detail from *Dress* 1994
spring/summer collection
from the Flying saucer collection
polyester, pleated and heat set
Purchased 1995   1995.781

The first fifty years of the twentieth century saw dramatic changes emerging in fashion each decade; for example, tightly laced garments with long skirts in the 1900s, and short dresses with few undergarments in the 1920s. The new distinctive styles radically changed people's lives, and they also reflected the new directions in society, such as the changing roles of women, and the social and economic effects of war. These modifications were extraordinary, and until the 1960s such major fashion changes occurred each decade, making the fashions of the previous decade totally unacceptable.

The Parisian haute couture fashion system caters for an elite clientele, and haute couture was worn mainly by women over forty. Its expense and the time-consuming nature of its fabrication and fittings puts it out of the reach of all but the wealthiest and most dedicated people. Its limited edition numbers of garments are not only expensive, but also beautifully made. They often take hundreds of hours' work using fabric and trims manufactured exclusively for the couturier for one season only.

The 'trickle down' theory suggests that haute couture strikes a much wider audience than just the original clientele, as over the following years the couture styles are copied for the mass markets and become fashion trends. This trend was at its most powerful during the 1950s, when designers such as Christian Dior and Cristobal Balenciaga

had an enormous influence over styles of women's clothing.

Not only were their creations immortalised in influential fashion magazines such as *Vogue*, *Harper's Bazaar* and *L'Officiel*, but they also made front-page newspaper and television news. After 'The New Look' women en mass followed the many changes in hemlines, shape and colours that the few fashion dictators produced. Other influences at work were subject to the enormous influence of the Parisian couturier and a ready-to-wear system based on producing cheaper, watered-down versions for the masses.

By the late 1950s the nature and sources of fashion began to change. Dress began to lose its formality. For example, the protocol concerning the wearing of hats and gloves began to be ignored. The style conventions for day and eveningwear became less obvious, as did the distinctions between formal and informal styles for daywear. Department stores, established since the mid nineteenth century, offered garments that were available ready-made.

By 1960, antiquated buying schedules and mail order services that often resulted in garments being unavailable were out of step with new market trends. Slowness to respond to new fashions and changes in buying patterns resulted in poor retail sales to young people.

Ready-to-wear or *prêt-à-porter* fashion came to dominate the fashion system. During the 1950s and 1960s independent fashion shops known as boutiques brought the latest design trends to a wider audience. In contrast to couture, ready-to-wear clothing is made in standard sizes and can be purchased in one visit to a boutique. The boutique specialised in a particular type of fashion or client, often with new ranges being produced every six weeks. Originally the name boutique derived from the small shops on the Left Bank in Paris which sold clothes of their own design. As couture sales dropped, and ready-to wear made profits, perfume and related accessory products became the means whereby the couture shows were financed.

In 1960 eleven Parisian couturiers formed a separate group and showed *prêt-à-porter* clothing two weeks before the couture collections. Their garments were made in standard sizes, to be mass produced and retailed through designer boutiques to cater for a broader market. By 1963, *stylistes* or ready-to-wear designers started producing new clothes, based not on an elite's desire for something extravagant and new but on what it was thought women wanted for a working lifestyle. The *stylistes* were first launched by French fashion magazines and became an instant success with foreign buyers. Designers such as Emmanuelle Khan and Karl Lagerfeld became famous as makers of ready-to-wear, and *prêt-à-porter* shows became a regular event in Paris, held after the couture parades.

As travel became easier and communications advanced, internationalism gradually became a prominent feature of the fashion industry. New fashion centres developed away from Paris, the traditional fashion city.

In Italy major catwalk parades were staged during the 1950s. Florence hosted the first Italian fashion show in 1951, held in the presence of the best-known foreign journalists and buyers. The extraordinary success of this event paved the way for regular parades to be held, later relocating to Milan, to showcase Italian fashion design and precipitate the major influence of Italian fashion from Pucci, Missoni, Armani and Versace.

Parades in New York, then later London Fashion Week and many similar events, broke the centuries-old monopoly that France had had on fashion. As affordable fashion became normal, men and women expressed their individuality through fashion choice: the designer's name came to represent a style or image that people could adopt.

Menswear also started to evolve from the 1950s onwards. By 1960 designers famous for making women's clothes, such as Pierre Cardin, began working on male collections. Traditionally men's clothes were made by tailors and dominated by the suit. In the 1960s designers began to take an interest in men's clothes as a fashion rather than as a uniform with very few variations. Starting in the 1950s, various sub-culture groups such as the British Teddy Boys and the Rockers developed distinctive forms of dress away from the mainstream. Street clothing, garments worn by particular sub-cultures, became a powerful force and stylistic influence opposing traditional clothing patterns. In a 'trickle up' effect, this form of clothing influences and provides major style sources for the ready-to-wear and couture designers. Multiculturalism and the power of the information super highway ensure that these influences spread rapidly over a global network.

In the 1960s there was also a revolution in social values. Young people had good disposable incomes, the feminist movement was growing, and the needs of career women and the use of the contraceptive pill had an impact on the authority of fashion. Other new factors began to exert an enormous influence over clothing styles. They included pop music, television and the large youth population who wanted their dress to state their difference from their parents. The notion emerged that people could wear whatever they liked, which exerted immense pressure on designers to come up with modern ideas, since people were prepared to engage with new looks year after year.

Neverthless, the idea that the demise of the significance of haute couture clothing marked the end of all true fashion is simply irrelevant. This is because the duality of fashion cannot be ignored: it is easily possible to admire a garment because it is unique, and also to admire a garment and its success because it is worn by lots of people.

The title *Couture to Chaos* suggests that fashion now comes from a variety of sources. Freedom of choice and diversity abound, often resulting in a confusion of looks. This does not imply a negative environment but rather, one that is a stimulating, fertile pool of ideas. Each designer now produces individual styles season by season, not just a signature look for each decade.

The museum environment

Displaying fashion in an art gallery can lead people to criticise exhibition technique and say that the display looks dead, that clothing needs to be seen on a living person otherwise it looks awful, or that the exhibition looks like a shop window display. They may comment, such as 'I wish I could see it moving'. Elizabeth Wilson, in her essay 'Fashion and the Postmodern body', describes the scene at the Pierre Cardin exhibition at the Victoria & Albert Museum, London, thus:

Strangest of all were the dead white sightless mannequins staring fixedly ahead, turned as if to stone in the middle of a decisive movement ... But without the living body they could not be said to fully exist. Without movement, they become oddly abstract and faintly uncanny.[10]

Comments about faces and rigor mortis are constantly expressed. And yet nobody at a decorative arts display worries that no tea is in the teapot or flowers in the vase. Nobody complains that painting and sculpture are shown in galleries, out of their original context. In displaying fashion we use a figure as a support system for something worthy of close examination, not as a personality.

People also complain about the low light levels at exhibitions of garments, which make it difficult to see the items. The effect of light on textiles is cumulative and so the light level is restricted by using filters and fixing its intensity at 70 lux. This is a standard museum practice that also applies to paper and other organic artefacts

Journalists and art critics who have never before seriously considered writing about fashion seem to find it easier to dismiss garments and restrict their commentary to the display mechanisms. For those who work professionally with fashion, years of listening to and reading fashion hype and public relations jargon make any serious dialogue seem irrelevant, and when a garment is no longer the fashion of the moment, we lose the ability to see the pieces, to understand the creative idea of the garment, and therefore we ignore or ridicule it.

But the mere survival of a garment does not confer legitimacy upon it, since it might always have been a poor example. Each garment has a story and it is our job to decipher this, to understand its meaning and, for an outstanding garment, to realise its importance. The study of fashion is not an exercise in nostalgia.

Of course the social meanings of clothes come into play, but clothing in a museum is never worn once it becomes part of the collection. The wearer provides part of the garment's provenance but it is rarely considered of primary importance. Our role is to represent and document the major moments in fashion and the work of the major artists involved in this art. Our acceptance of an item into the collection aims to ensure that this garment survives for future generations to appreciate.

PACO RABANNE, Paris est. c. 1966
Paco Rabanne, designer
Spain born 1934
Evening dress c. 1969
aluminium jersey, silk grosgrain ribbon
Purchased 1994   CT425-1994

We hope to provide our audience with material for new interpretations and discourses about fashion, but we must also understand the role of the museum or art gallery. We are not a department store, working wonders of visual merchandising. We are restricted in display methods due to the inherent fragility of fashion items, the need to conserve them and our commitment to preservation. On the other hand, no amount of film footage or photographic images will give us the vision we see, when a Paco Rabanne gold metallic mesh sheath dress is exhibited hugging a display form. We want to enable people to view at close hand the visual aesthetics of a garment, distancing themselves from a personality or face, and to appreciate the various meanings and signals the garment generates. A high-tech armour of shimmering gold? A triumph of design and manufacture? A sexual lure, or a sculpture masterpiece? One can only ponder.

Retro clothing ignites memories and contemporary works can incite reactions of horror or disbelief. To be affected or influenced by a garment, we do not need to wear it. Costume should inspire us and colour our world.

We must learn to acknowledge and be aware of the various qualities of artists working in fashion, and embrace the aesthetics, function and form of these works, not only as wearers but as viewers or visitors to an art gallery.

Notes

1   Elizabeth Wilson, *Adorned in dreams: fashion and modernity*, Virago, London, 1985, p. 60.

2   Richard Martin & Harold Koda, *Flair*, Fashion Institute of Technology, Rizzoli, New York, 1992, p. 19.

3   Elizabeth Wilson, 'All the Rage', from *Fabrications: costume and the female body*, Jane Gaines & Charlotte Herzog (eds), Routledge, London, 1990, p. 28.

4   Colin McDowell, *Dressed to kill*, Hutchinson, London, 1994, p. 8.

5   Nicholas Coleridge, *The fashion conspiracy*, William Heinemann Ltd, London, 1988, p. 6.

6   Ingrid Sischy & Germano Celant, Editorial, *Artforum*, New York, 1982, p. 35.

7   Annette Tapert, 'For collectors: Beverley Birks/Assembling the finest of 20th century Haute Couture', *Architectural Digest*, October 1994, p. 40.

8   McDowell, op.cit., p.8.

9   Ted Polhemus, *Bodystyles*, Leonard Publishing, London, 1988, p. 136.

10 Elizabeth Wilson, 'Fashion and the Postmodern Body', from *Chic thrills*, Juliet Ash & Elizabeth Wilson (eds), Pandora Press, London, 1992.

UNITED STATES
Designer unknown
Detail from *Souper dress* c. 1967
wood pulp, cotton: non-woven, screenprint
Purchased 1991   CT76-1991

The Wham, Wham, Wow Way[1] — aspects of Pop and futuristic inspired fashions in the 1960s

In the 1960s fashion experienced the rejection of the gradual evolution of a particular style, and instead sought new and innovative clothing forms such as the mini, trousers and boots made from the latest, often synthetic materials, in large, bold, often dazzling optical patterns and vibrant colours. Designers looked forward, seeking inspiration from speculation about the future. This led to the breaking of traditional rules of fashion, and the wilful mixing of styles, pattern, shape and even sexual demarcations with a crazy abandonment and individualism.

The hierarchy of fashion was challenged and defeated with the rise of the boutique and mass produced clothing. Space exploration, advanced technology and an obsession with the future and improvement of one's lifestyle gave rise to a bold creative rationale and pressure to develop innovative and experimental garments.

The youth population needed clothing that suited a more informal lifestyle than their parents had ever known. 'Pop' fashion epitomises a celebration of youth, new technologies and original clothing ideas. It displays a total disregard for time-consuming making processes, ornate draperies, delicate embroideries and expensive jewels. Fashion is created for now, not tomorrow and never forever. Pop culture was: 'For the most part non-reflective, non-didactic, dedicated only to pleasure ... to catch[ing] the spirit of the time and translat[ing] this into objects, fashion and music.'[2]

The values of the emerging youth culture were primarily expressed in pop music. American Bob Dylan epitomised the moral and social protest of the time, with lyrics like:

Come, mothers and fathers, throughout the land,
And con't criticise what you can't understand.
Your sons and your daughters are beyond your
command.
Your old world is rapidly ageing.
Please get out of the new one if you can't lend
your hand,
For the times, they are a-changing.[3]

The needs of a new youth market led to designers creating garments unlike any a couturier had conceived before, which were suitable for 1960s young people to wear: clothing types like mini dresses, hot pants, jumpsuits and trousers. The form of these garments now often looks too familiar for us to appreciate their radical origins, and needs to be understood in the context of complex 1950s clothing designed for older women. The large youth population needed different clothing that embraced their ideas and, like music, gave them a means of expression. Clothing for them did not even follow the traditional categories of day, evening, formal, casual or even seasonal wear.

Advances in textile technology provided the designer with new raw materials and new technologies in fibre, dyes, finishes, and fasteners that resulted in some startling visual effects and production methods. The excitement and allure of the future inspired designers to experiment with alternatives to their standard materials. Paper, polyurethane coatings, acrylic and Velcro fastenings had a new range of visual and practical applications.

It is as impossible to be led by the past when working with new materials as it is to know how these materials will survive or evolve in a museum. Certain materials do change with age: white vinyl that yellows, polyurethane that cracks and acrylic that loses its shape are of concern. And yet the initial effect of these materials in garments is fresh and totally new. These ultramodern synthetic materials offered short cuts in cleaning. Traditional materials and complex constructions required laborious and expensive cleaning methods, while new concepts such as drip dry, permanent press and non-iron were alluring and saleable features of the new synthetic fabrics.

The nature of this type of fashion challenges the museum environment. The permanence of art and our concern to slow up the disintegration process in order to allow works to be enjoyed for hundreds of years to come is at odds with the purpose of many of these garments. In a museum we study everything in the context of preserving it for the future and maintaining it in as pristine condition as possible. This becomes a complex issue when we work against the artist's original intention, when we deal with costumes that are disposable or actually intended to decompose and fall apart. All we can do is slow up the process of disintegration and stabilise the work.

A garment we observe now may be poorly constructed, of poor quality materials, initially fabricated in twenty minutes, affordable to young buyers and designed to be worn only momentarily. A garment such as this reflects the spirit of the times and should be considered and appreciated with the contmeporary ideas of the costume in mind, rather than the construction finish and issues of longevity.

Youth was also represented by the young designers, who were the creative forces of this decade. It is significant that the management of the major French couture house Christian Dior appointed as chief designer the twenty-two-year-old Yves Saint Laurent (France born 1936) after the death of its founder

MARIMEKKO, Helsinki est. 1951
Armi Ratia, founder
Finland 1912–1979
Maiji Isola, chief textile designer
Finland born 1927
Mini dress c. 1967
cotton, screenprint
Anonymous gift 1977 D25-1977

MARY QUANT, London est. 1955
GINGER GROUP from 1963
Mary Quant, designer
Great Britain born 1934
Detail from *Mini dress* c. 1963
rayon
Gift of Joanna Motion 1996   1996.119

in 1957. Youth now inspired culture. Unlike his predecessor, Yves Saint Laurent did not look to the nineteenth century for inspiration, but to the popular culture of the Beat Generation and to the kids on the street. Recalling the reaction of the audience to one of his first couture parades in 1960, Yves Saint Laurent wrote:

Motorcycle jackets in alligator, mink coats with sweater sleeves, turtleneck collars under finely cut flannel suits — those street inspirations all seem very inelegant to a lot of people sitting on the gilt chairs of a couture salon. But this was the first collection in which I tried hard for poetic expression in my clothes. The Street had a new pride, its own chic, and I found the street inspiring as I would often again.[4]

Too short

The original 'mini' is now synonymous with 1960s youth culture and its visual form most readily identifiable with this era. However it was not a new clothing form. 'Mini' is a French term originally used to describe a skirt length reaching to mid thigh, and it became the term to describe the 1960s fashion style of very simple clothes in brief lengths. This style revolution initially appeared in the 1920s with short straight dresses. The difference here was the interpretation, especially the inexpensive materials, form of decoration and construction methods. All these are innovative.

The shift dress of the 1920s was a new fashion, providing a radical alternative and contrast to the ornate and heavy garments, worn with complex undergarments, of the Edwardian era. The form of these usually fragile garments was very basic and the most exciting examples were covered entirely with a casing of sequins or glass beads, creating stunning optical effects. These dresses represent the *garçonne* look which can be interpreted as the least or the most provocative style of dress. Like the 1920s, the 1960s celebrated youth and rebellion. The mini, like the *garçonne* style, was a symbol of youth and freedom from the shackles of the complex clothing worn by your parents. The mini was symbolic of women in control of their own destiny and bodies. Legs exposed and unencumbered allowed women greater freedom in movement. The contraceptive pill now allowed them sexual liberation and the right to choose their sexual partner.

The construction of the mini was minimal; its visual impact became its most important or novel feature, especially when translated in plastic, metal or paper. The mini accelerated the development of tights, initially for warmth and then as an alternative to stockings and suspenders which could be seen easily. When wearing these garments 'The fashionable posture was a mixture of modesty and exhibitionism: knees together facing slightly inwards and feet wide apart'.[5]

Mary Quant (Great Britain born 1934) is perhaps the most famous of the advocates of the mini skirt. In 1966 she wrote:

Over and over again I was told I was responsible for the off-beat clothes that became known as the Chelsea Look. I heard my clothes described as dishy, grotty, geary, kinky, mod, poove and all the rest of it. People either loved or hated them. But, in fact, no one designer is ever responsible for such a revolution. All a designer can do is to anticipate a mood before people realise that they are bored with what they have already got.[6]

Quant responded like many of her generation to the rejection of the idealised ultrafemininity of the 1940s and 1950s, dresses with stiffened skirts and stiletto heels, garments more in tune with a nineteenth-century image of a woman and her role in society. Fashion had not been designed with a young person in mind, requiring as it did hats, gloves, ballgowns, suits — garments that demand protocol, formality and time to dress.

Mary Quant studied Art at Goldsmith's College of Art, London, and met Alexander Plunkett Greene whom she married in 1957. In 1955 Quant, Greene and Archie McNair opened the first Bazaar boutique in the King's Road, London. When Quant could not find appropriate stock for the shop she began designing her own range of garments. She 'created clothes that ... allowed people to run, to leap, to retain their precious freedom'.[7]

Quant also advocated the use of synthetic fabrics and machine-made garments: 'what a machine is capable of doing itself instead of making it copy what the hand does'.

The *Mini dress* (c. 1963) looks like a little girl's party frock, introducing the theme of the child-woman and accentuating the look of the very young. The dress in white rayon has a scoop neckline and plunging back, and is trimmed with a double ruffle around the neckline and hem. The dress has a back zip fastener trimmed with a bow to hide the top of the fastener. Produced under the Ginger

Group label, this garment was inexpensive and affordable to a younger clientele.

The Finnish designer Armi Ratia (Finland 1912–1979) once described herself as a fashion hater. She started the Printex company in Helsinki, producing bold, colourful printed textiles which later expanded into clothing with the Marimekko label.

Ratia created the Marimekko clothing and textile range as an alternative to current styles from the fashion establishment. Her works were designed for a particular lifestyle — not a constantly changing fashionable one, but one to satisfy the needs of women who wanted informal and intelligent clothing.

The Marimekko dresses, though originally designed for a limited audience, are perhaps the

prototypes of the *jeune fille* look. In Finnish the word Marimekko means 'little girl's dress for Mary'.

These garments were popular particularly in America. They were described in *American Fabrics* magazine as 'clothes with the overtones of architecture rather than couture, simple but colourful, clothes for fun'.[8]

Marimekko garments were usually produced in cotton and were trans-seasonal and multi-purpose. The most distinctive feature were the large-scale non-figurative graphic prints, in bold contrasting colours. The basic fit of a Marimekko garment is determined largely by the shoulders, with most of the dresses designed to fall loosely to the hem. This elementary construction enhanced the striking oversized prints and also made the clothes convenient and comfortable to wear.

Huge screenprinted circles in shades of pink cover the sleeveless *Mini dress* (c. 1967). The only interruption to the pattern is the line of machine sewing around the semi-circular inset pockets. Another version, *Mini dress* (c. 1967), has a zipper down the front and literally glows with a pulsating optical wave pattern in crimson and green.

POSTER DRESS, London
Harry Gordon, designer
'Eye' poster dress 1968
wood pulp, cotton: non-woven,
screenprint, Velcro
Label, screenprinted, black on white:
POSTER DRESS
Purchased 1991   CT77-1991

Throwaways

The American artist Andy Warhol helped create the aesthetic of Pop dress. Following the notion that anybody could do anything, young inexperienced designers created garments from man-made materials such as vinyl which would look great but disintegrate after a few weeks of wear, and so could never become out-of-date. The phenomenon of 'no name' clothing lessened the cult of the designer and broadened the accessibility of fashion.

The use of paper for clothing originated with the American Scott paper company, which sold paper dresses through the mail for $US1.25 as a promotional exercise for their fancy paper napkins.

Rows of Campbell Soup cans emblazoned across the *Souper dress* (c. 1967) recall the most famous of Pop art icons. The dress was inspired by Warhol's famous series of paintings, originally displayed in the Ferus Gallery in Los Angeles in 1962. The paintings depicted rows of stacked soup cans in all their varieties just as they might appear on a supermarket shelf.

This paper dress integrates the new Pop art movement with fashion and amusement. It arouses public awareness of an artist such as Warhol and

brings art into everyday life. A sleeveless American A-line mini dress, the *Souper* dress has no fastening mechanisms and was simply slipped over the head. This dress confronts the viewer with processed food and a machine-age repetition.

One of the major design concerns about paper dresses was their flammability. People feared that one cigarette at a party could inflame the wearer. However, by law the material had to be treated with a fire retardant. This resulted in the rather bizarre care labels stating 'NO CLEANING NO WASHING ITS CAREFREE FIRE RESISTANT UNLESS WASHED OR CLEANED'.

All told, disposable apparel fits a need and a mood of present-day living. Who indeed wants anything that will last forever?[9]

'Paper' clothes had a brief run among the trendy during 1966–68. Inexpensive, disposable, very fashionable, these paper garments appealed to the adventurous and young people, and provided a fun alternative to traditional dress. Throw-away garments were hailed as the clothing of the coming decades. The American fashion designer John Weitz predicted in 1967 that:

Disposable clothes are definitely the thing of the future ... self-service vending machines will probably be the answer. It's no use getting sentimental about clothes.[10]

The new non-woven material used for these clothes, often referred to as paper or as a short life textile or a web fabric, is produced like felt by a binding process with wood pulp and rayon mesh. It was very inexpensive because it involved no spun threads or weaving. The fibres were held together by bonding agents, self-fusing of

thermoplastic fibres or needle punching to interlock the threads.

Stern brothers in New York advertised paper fabrics at 99 cents per yard, perfect to 'Whip up disposable evening dresses! Zowie discotheque — cover-ups! Snappy tent dresses! Mini — over-the bikini cover dresses!'[11]

Another example of the paper dress genre was a series of Poster dresses designed by the American graphic artist Harry Gordon. These were produced in five designs: a cat, a rose, an eye, a rocket taking off, a hand with the palm open in the Buddhist

UNITED STATES
Designer unknown
Detail from *Souper dress* c. 1967
wood pulp, cotton: non-woven, screenprint
Purchased 1991   CT76-1991

FRANÇOIS VILLON, Paris
White leather knee high boots c. 1967
leather, elastic, PVC plastic
Gift of Miss Sheila Scotter AM MBE 1995
1995.315.a-b

peace sign gesture, and an Allen Ginsberg poem. 'Put-on Posters' sold for $US3.00 each.

A beautiful female eye with curled eyelashes looks out at the viewer from the *'Eye' poster dress* (1968). A sleeveless, A-line mini dress fastened at the left shoulder with Velcro strips, the dress is dominated by a black and white photographic blow-up image of an eye. The screen-printed design in large dots depicts an enlargement of an image originally from the offset lithographic process. When worn, the dress took on the form of a wearable poster.

This dress is made from the non-woven material Kyron, manufactured by Kimberley Stevens in the United States. This fabric, made from 75 per cent rayon and 25 per cent nylon, was bonded on both sides and washable, with a life of three to four wears. To shorten the dress, just cut.

Today paper garments are used in hospitals as an efficient disposable garment, but as a fashion concept they were short lived.

Severe. Function.

From the traditional training ground of haute couture the fashion designer André Courrèges (France born 1923) created some of the most extreme silhouettes of this period, using advanced tailoring skills. Working in Paris for Cristobal Balenciaga from 1952 to 1960 as a cutter, he had mastered the intricacies and complexity of 1950s dress when he opened his own house in 1961. Courrèges was to become known as the couturier of the space age. Not an advocate of the quickly made or disposable garments of the 1960s, Courrèges used the new technology and spirit of

COURREGES, Paris est. 1961
André Courrèges
France born 1923
Mini tunic and skinny rib top c. 1969
cotton, polyurethane, polymide, Spandex, nylon, metal snap fasteners, metal hooks and eyes
Gift of Mary Lipshut 1983 CT108a-b-1983

the day to improve the quality of tailored garments and altered their nature and construction.

He designed clothes for the 'contemporary' woman. By 1964 he was designing mini A-line dresses worn with flat-heeled boots or shoes.

The *White leather knee high boots* (c. 1967) by François Villon, with a clear plastic upper shoe, were designed as an accessory for Courrèges' space age collections. The leg section has a

square lattice work of leather strips elasticised under the horizontal sections, allowing the boot to hug the leg. The boot has the new square toe to balance a very low heel. These would be worn with coloured or metallic pantyhose and a mini outfit.

Courrèges' clothes were minimally decorated, usually in one colour and tailored. Journalists used adjectives such as 'hardness', 'toughness', 'severe', and 'anti-feminine' to describe his clothing designs, and referred to him as the 'Le Corbusier

COURREGES, Paris est. 1961
André Courrèges
France born 1923
Trouser suit 1972
comprising coat, knit top and trousers
polyurethane-coated cotton, acrylic
Purchased 1995   1995.780.a-c

The *Black mini tunic* (c. 1969) is made from a synthetic membrane of polyurethane coating on a cotton knit ground. In time the coating eventually cracks and a white cloudy film appears on the surface as a result of a chemical reaction that was not known at the time. The surface simulates leather and the image is tough or kinky. This garment can be taken off in seconds by means of a system of practical snap fasteners. The straps are attached to the dress by four snap fasteners each and the dress fastens at the side with six snap fasteners. The belt is also attached by a snap fastener. This belt has a metal buckle with the distinctive Courrèges logo.

The tunic is worn with a white acrylic *skinny rib top* that clings to the body. This is a tough-looking garment with hard-edge qualities which exudes a sense of power and confrontation from its pure structure.

Perhaps Courrèges' most significant fashion development was the introduction and advocacy of trousers as a standard form of women's dress. This became a major trend from the 1960s onwards with the development of unisex fashions.

Courrèges announced that:

the woman of 1964 still dresses as in 1925. A modern woman wants to work, travel, even run. She can't do these things properly in a skirt. We are experimenting with trousers to find a new way of dressing which fits the age.'[13]

He promoted pants for evening and daywear worn with flat-heeled shoes or boots.

The intensity of colour in the orange *Trouser suit* (1972) is quite overwhelming, the wet look coat with matching hipster pants contrasted against a white skinny rib top. The coat, with its ultra bright synthetic surface of polyurethane-coated cotton, has a contrasting stark white collar and a white felt piqued edging along the shoulders, sleeves and cuffs. An arm band on the left arm carries the logo. This also fastens with snap fasteners. A white acrylic short-sleeved top celebrates the use of a synthetic fibre, which was a cheaper alternative to wool and easily dyed to produce hot, rich colours. It could be washed in a washing machine with ordinary detergent and tumbled dry. The orange acrylic knit hipster flares feature the new permanent press technology down the front of the leg. The impact of permanent press technology, which arrived in 1964, was limited until the early 1970s,

of the Paris couture' because of the stark forms and architectural quality of his work. It is difficult to express in words the minimalist aesthetic, common in other contemporary art forms, as it applies to fashion. Everything is stripped back to basics with solid blocks of colour, black or white, thus breaking from accepted forms of couture clothing that used certain types of fabrics, decoration, and characteristics that were considered feminine: chiffon, embroidery, frills, flowing skirts and puffed sleeves.

FRANCE

Designer unknown

Evening dress and hotpants 1967

wool flannel, plastic sequins, cotton

bobble trim

Gift of Mary Lipshut 1984

CT143A-B-1984

when a new heat set process that worked well with synthetic fabrics was developed.

Trousers became an integral part of the female wardrobe. Previously they had been seen as avant-garde, experimental or simple at-home wear.

Formerly part of the male wardrobe, trousers became a symbol of liberation and equality. At first their general acceptance was slow. During the 1960s in Australia many recreational clubs and restaurants turned away fashion-conscious women wearing trousers, because they did not adhere to the standard dress codes which insisted that the female patrons wear skirts or dresses, NO PANTS.

Fashion is for fun. This is a new era. No one is interested any more in how clothes are cut ... No one cares. No one wants to be elegant, sophisticated, raffine. All that is out! Fun and sex are in. The wedding dress is out — the divorcing dress in.[14]

A purge in traditional clothing types and values was occurring.

Perhaps the most challenging garments created were those that used alternative construction methods. Paco Rabanne rejected standard joining and sewing techniques in his garments from plastic, glass or metal. Rabanne (Spain born 1934) studied architecture and his mother worked for Balenciaga.

PACO
Paco Rabanne, designer
Made by C. Unglik, France
Sandal c. 1970
inject moulded plastic, leather,
ridged rubber
Gift of Mary Lipshut 1995
1995.490a-b

PACO
Paco Rabanne, designer
Made by C. Unglik, France
Sandal c. 1970
inject moulded plastic, leather,
ridged rubber
Gift of Mary Lipshut 1984
CT134-1984

He began as a designer of accessories before opening his Parisian couture house in 1961. One of the most adventurous designers ever, he used plastic or metal discs joined together by metal links rather than sewing.

I defy anyone to design a hat, coat or dress that hasn't been done before ... The only new frontier left in fashion is the finding of new materials.[15]

The *Evening dress* (c. 1969) is made up of tiny gold-coloured metal platelets forming a jersey type material which drapes and clings to the body. The dress is incredibly heavy but once fastened it tightly moulds the body in its shimmering reflective surface. The bodice has only one sleeve and from under the sleeveless arm extends a long sash that can be wrapped around the body in various ways, creating sparkling effects of sculptural drapery — soft folds with a hard surface.

Rabanne's shoe designs with their strong sculptural shapes were also extreme. *Sandals* (c. 1970), in

white leather with four crossover straps, have inject moulded plastic soles with six elevated sections.

Sandals (c. 1970), in orange leather with two crossover straps, have inject moulded plastic soles forming two elevated sections with rubber soles.

Hot pants were so named by the American fashion magazine *Women's Wear Daily* in early 1971 to describe women's short shorts, often made of leather or luxury fabrics, worn with coloured tights and fancy tops as evening wear and daringly worn on the city streets from about 1965. *Evening dress and hotpants* (1967) in grey flannel is decorated with large silver plastic sequins in flower shapes and trimmed with a black cotton bobble trim. The dress is high waisted and open from the waist down. This is an interesting mix of materials, especially in the use of the flannel.

In this period the length of garments became excessive and eclectic. No one length was the norm and they were mixed indiscriminately. From 1968 the term 'Maxi' was used to describe long garments worn during the day, and 'Midi' described garments stopping at mid-calf.

Strong patterns, violently clashing colours, colours that practically glowed in the dark, the psychedelic pinks, purples, oranges, greens and yellows, in wild shapes that simulated a drug experience, were used on all forms of graphic and decorative art.

The fashion status symbol of the 1960s was the Pucci look, dresses, pants and shirts printed in wild colours in complex heraldic-style patterns. Emilio Pucci (Italy born 1914), known as The Marchese Pucci di Barsento, opened his workshop in Florence in 1949. By 1950 it opened as a fashion house called Emilio.

Pucci created some of the most startling and innovative prints, which still have an extraordinary impact. By combining oversized, complex patterns in brillant colours he reduced the garment to a simple backdrop.

PUCCI, Florence est. c. 1944
Emilio Pucci, designer
Italy born 1914
Palazzo jump suit c. 1968
silk, screenprint, fringing
Purchased 1993   CT6-1993

PIERRE BALMAIN, Paris est. 1946
Pierre Balmain, designer
France 1914–1984
Athenes evening ensemble c. 1970
silk organza, screenprint
Purchased 1995   1995.672a-b

Pulsating pattern Technicolour.

The psychedelic revolution grew out of the underground drug culture of hallucinogens such as LSD and the new spirit of aggressive questioning and challenging of the norm. From the mid 1950s and during the 1960s LSD was legally available and inexpensive. It was used particularly by intellectuals and artists, who experimented with its power to free the mind and allow ideas to flow. They inspired a technicolour movement, in design and music.

The combination of a shirt and trousers in one piece was novel, as the jump suit was initially designed for flyers during World War 1 and later expanded into sportswear, particularly for skiing and more recently astronauts' suits. Not until the 1960s did this style emerge as a multi-purpose easy/leisure style.

The *Palazzo jump suit* (c. 1968) is made of printed silk jersey with a deep V neck and front zipper, long sleeves and flared trousers trimmed with black fringing. The fabric is printed with an intricate abstract pattern of curvilinear forms and swirls combining an unusual palette of colors, with bright orange, pink, and black contrasted against pale pink, orange, grey and the palest green. The design is outlined with fine black lines. The interesting use of borders, common in Indian saris and Indonesian batik lengths, leads the pattern in various directions. Pucci travelled in 1960 to Bali

and was greatly inspired by Indonesian fabrics, particularly the border patterns and the sarong-style skirt. The fabric is printed and cut so that the pattern merges into the structure and flow of the garment.

The design of this fabric incorporates the artist's given name, Emilio. This device recurs in all his textiles and was done initially after a suggestion by Pucci's lawyer as a type of patent and method of copyright — just as other designers choose to use embroidered monograms or signature buttons.

It is interesting to note the use of the given name rather than the surname for this purpose, but as Pucci explained, 'it was considered shameful for a Pucci to work, and that is why I put only Emilio'.[16]

The black fringing of this jump suit moves with the wearer's movement, adding to the dynamic nature of this piece. These vibrant garments expressed the mood of the time and made their

MISSONI, Milan est. 1961
Emmanuelle Khanh
France born 1947
Pant suit 1966
comprising tunic and trousers
lurex, acrylic, machine knitted
Purchased 1996   1996.187.a-b

older wearers in particular feel up-to-date. The garments produced maximum impact with a minimum of sewing detailing.

As couture struggled to come to terms with the youth revolution some masterpieces were still created. Pierre Balmain (France 1914–1982) established his Paris couture house in 1946, after working for Molyneux, Lelong and Dior. Balmain was trained in architecture, and his garments are often a celebration in geometry, form and print.

Athenes evening ensemble (c. 1970) consisting of a full-length dress and a contoured wrap of silk organza printed in a multi-coloured geometric motif, was influenced by the contemporary minimalist art movement.

The dress is created from four multi-coloured geometric-style scarves designed by Balmain and entitled *'Athenes' scarf no. 146*. The construction of the dress ingeniously fuses these pieces together to create a continuous bold pattern. The garment is entirely hand finished and is stamped with the unique couture number '154593'.

The neckline, side seams and side fasteners are highlighted with a 5cm strip of black organza, sharply defining the conical shape of this dress. Its matching wrap consists of six pieces assembled in an irregular shape featuring two large triangular ends. The wrap can be draped around the dress in various ways to produce an interesting fusion of geometric elements.

During this period the status and styling of machine-knit garments extended beyond basic comfort items for outer and underwear, to become an influential fashion type. The juxtaposition of texture, colour and layering creates complex optical effects.

The Missonis resurrected knitwear from comfort wear into an exciting and innovative part of modern fashion. Tai Missoni (Jugoslavia born 1921) and Rosita Jelmini (Italy) married in 1953.

MISSONI, Milan est. 1953
Tai Missoni
Jugoslavia born 1921
Rosita Missoni
Italy
Pant suit 1971
spring/summer collection
comprising vest with belt, jumper and pants
wool, nylon; machine knitted
Gift of Mary Lipshut 1983   CT110-1983

Tai ran a business which specialised in producing tracksuits and sports wear, established in 1946. After his marriage the business expanded into fashion knitwear. Initially the Missonis used various designers until in 1967 Rosita was appointed the chief designer.

In 1966, on a catwalk at the Teatro Gerolamo in Milan, the Missonis presented their first collection, designed by Emmanuelle Khanh (France born 1937) from distinctive lurex fabrics.

Emmanuelle Khanh had begun her career as a fashion model at Balenciaga. Upset and disturbed by what she saw as the old-fashioned styling, her new look was known as 'the Droop', a very slim silhouette that clung to the body, often with scalloped collars, funnel sleeves and curvy hemlines. Khanh's collaboration with the Missonis combined her uninhibited style with their innovative knit fabrics.

The *Pant suit* (1966) has a sleeveless tunic with a ring halter neck, formed with scalloped bands of alternate colours in lime green and emerald green lurex over the hipster flared trousers in the lime green lurex.

This was the first Missoni garment imported into Australia by Meredith Imports of Melbourne. It was rejected by the buyers at Georges and Myer department stores as being too outrageous for the local market — 'Who would wear it?', they asked?

Missoni coordinated outfits which often consisted of three to five items, in related colours with various patterns, presenting a more casual style of clothing.

Pant suit (1971) consists of a vest in an Argyle pattern in cream, royal blue and three shades of green, with a matching tie belt and the front facing in broad stripes. This is juxtaposed with a short-sleeved knit top with diagonal stripes of

MR FREEDOM, London est. 1969
Tommy Roberts, founder
born 1942
Pamla Motown, chief designer
Pant suit 1971
comprising jacket, shirt and trousers
cotton, polyester
Gift of Jennifer Phipps 1978   D4c-1978

minute blue squares and cream dashes on a bright green ground, trimmed at the neckline and waist with shaded solid stripes in greens and blue.

The pants have wide legs with an elasticised waist, in a matching pattern of squares and dashes. This outfit was also imported into Australia by Meredith Imports. Australians would not buy the complete set, preferring to buy only one piece and mix it with plainer items. Referred to by the American fashion press as a 'put-together', this combination of dots and prints and different patterns and colours laid on top of one another matched and clashed at the same time. The optical effects are more challenging when seen in the light of pre-computer design and the changing status of knitwear. These are colourways and patterns that mix but do not match.

The name Mr Freedom invites a certain expectation of clothing that knew no boundaries. Founded by Tommy Roberts in 1969 on King's Road and relocated to Kensington High Street in 1970, Mr Freedom's happening-style clothes were designed by Pamla Motion. This clothing was inspired by cartoon characters, American sports gear and the work of various Pop artists and graphic designers. The look was young and very bright with big patterns.

The bright orange *Pant suit* (1971) is a garment to be noticed. The jacket has padded shoulders fitted with wide pointed lapels highlighted with large orange plastic buttons. The front features an optical pattern of semi-circular bands of black and yellow meeting at the waist, fastening with four orange buttons, and the pattern continues onto the back. The matching orange hipster jeans in sail cloth have contrast yellow top stitching.

By 1965 hippie dress had captured the youth audience with its anti-fashion philosophy and disregard for the new. People made their own personal fashion statements by combining exotic multicultural (ethnic) garments with denim jeans, jewellery, long hair and unisex looks. Hippies rejected the recent synthetic fabrics and anything that was brand new and sought their clothing in flea markets or the cottage craft industry. Denim jeans, originally worn by farmers and workmen in the nineteenth century, were revived in the 1960s with flared legs. Denim was to become the staple clothing item for the next three decades.

Notes

1   From the quote 'Wow! Explode! The sixties it came to life in a pure, exaggerated, crazed-out, wham, wham, wow way' by the American designer Betsey Johnson. In Valerie Steele, *Women of fashion: twentieth-century designers*, Rizzoli, New York, 1991.

2   George Melly, *Revolt into style*, Cox & Wynam Ltd, London, 1970, p. 154.

3   'The times they are a changing' first released by CBS Records Inc., USA, 1964.

4   *Yves Saint Laurent*, Metropolitan Museum of Art, Thames & Hudson, London, 1984, p. 20.

5   Nigel Whiteley, *Pop design: Modernism to Mod*, Design Council, London, 1987, p. 104.

6   Mary Quant, *Quant by Quant*, Redwood Press Ltd, London, 1966, p. 75.

7   ibid.

8   'Design research is a way of life', Young world of fabrics and fashions, *American Fabrics*, number 71, Spring/Summer 1966, p. 58.

9   'Throwaway clothes on the March', *American Fabrics*, number 73, Fall/Winter 1966, p. 6.

10 Rodney Bennett-England, *Dress optional — the revolution in menswear*, Peter Owen, London, 1967, p. 99.

11 'Non-wovens & paper — the web textiles', *American Fabrics*, number 76, Summer 1967, p. 69.

12 Alexander Palmer, 'Paper clothes: not just a fad' from *Dress and popular culture*, Patricia A. Cunningham and Susan Voso Lab (eds), 1991, p. 91.

13 Anne Ryan, 'Space age fashion Courrèges & Ungaro', Ruth Lynam (ed.), *Couture*, Doubleday & Co., New York, 1972, p. 201.

14 'Go Go International', *American Fabrics*, number 71, Spring/Summer 1966, p. 49.

15 Joel Lobenthal, *Radical rags: fashions of the sixties*, Abbeville Press, New York, 1990, p. 63.

16 Shirley Kennedy, *Pucci: a renaissance in fashion*, Abbeville Press, New York, 1991, p. 73.

BIBA, London 1963–1975, reopened 1978, reopened 1994
Barbara Hulanicki, designer
Poland born 1936
Detail from *Men's suit* c. 1969
cotton corduroy, nylon
Presented by Rodney DeSoos 1995
1995.702a-c

On the other side of the past[1] — nostalgia, the 1970s

By 1969 the first US astronauts had stood on the moon and the world discussed with excitement the possibilities of further space exploration. However designers and wearers, motivated by the future and its challenges in seeking ways to improve life in the 1960s, also played their part in triggering a strong backlash, resulting in a total rejection of everything new and a fear of the unknown.

A sense of disillusionment and dissatisfaction with contemporary culture and the too rapid pace of change occurred in the late 1960s. The Vietnam war, the Six Day war in the Middle East, the construction of the Berlin Wall, the cultural revolution in China, the assassinations of President Kennedy and Martin Luther King, major riots and the build up of nuclear weapons throughout the world caused many people to fear the future. People escaped to the past for alternatives, to a time zone perceived as simpler, safer and closer to nature than the present.

In fashion this translated into retro, nostalgic fashions designed to look like those of decades or centuries earlier and folk costumes or garments found in second-hand shops. The rapid and extreme fashion changes in the 1960s lead in some quarters to a total rejection of fluctuations in clothing styles, and a transition from futuristic looks to romantic attire. The fashion upheavals of the 1960s confronted traditional fashion norms and the mini and trousers successfully made all other garments look old fashioned and out-of-date. Fashion artists begin to carve strong individual signature looks. Australian designers also started

to emerge during this period, responding to and stimulated by their local environment to create unique styles.

General world instability continued throughout the 1970s. The Cambodian war, civil wars in Lebanon, Angola and Cyprus, the growing cost of fossil fuels, general concerns about the environment and the extraordinary impact of colour television, transmitting news and popular culture, reinforced people's feelings of uncertainty and distrust of future trends. The value and meaning of clothing had also changed, and this culminated by 1976 with the emergence of punk culture, a rejection of all current clothing values.

The old notion of fashion was challenged when designers began to create timeless clothes, intending that they could be worn for twenty or thirty years. Types of garments emerged that were not constantly reinvented to look out-of-date; only minor details changed. Colin McDowell has said of this trend: 'A look that is worn and copied for several years without any significant change or evolution is not fashion: it is a mode of dress'.[2]

In terms of fashion, where does this leave us in the late twentieth century? Or has the nature and definition of fashion evolved to the point where the days of extreme change are over? After all, we no longer see a new style produced every season, only variations produced by so many different designers.

Retrospect. Reconstruct. Resurrect. The past.

Set in a fake antique-style interior that had the atmosphere of an exotic bazaar, the London Biba boutique opened in 1964. It was cluttered with old chairs, potted palms and bursting at the seams with feather boas, lurex, coloured pantyhose and lots of very inexpensive clothes.

During the 1960s and 1970s Barbara Hulanicki (Poland born 1936) and her husband Stephen Fitz-Simon created a shop, look and attitude towards style known as Biba, the name of Hulanicki's younger sister.

Hulanicki studied fashion at the Brighton School of Art and began her career as a fashion artist. She started a small mail order fashion business and its success led her to open this boutique, in Abingdon Road, London. Biba dress is influenced by garments of the past and expresses an idealised romantic image or nostalgic mood 'having more to do with the current idea of what they were like than reality'.

Biba sold clothes inspired by the Art Nouveau and Art Deco periods, often in dark colours such as plum, prune and black, using old-fashioned fabrics such as satin, velvet or crepe, and delicate and romantic floral prints. In 1968 John McConnell designed the black and gold Biba logo inspired by Celtic imagery.

These clothes were very cheap and not necessarily well made. The garments often looked like fancy dress clothes and previous styles of dress, such as the 'granny' dress, designed to simulate the clothes worn by grandmother.

The *Granny dress* (c. 1968), in a dark green and beige floral patterned chiffon, evokes the styling of the Edwardian age. Its high choker collar, bishop sleeves and covered buttons are elements associated with that period. However this semi-transparent garment worn without its traditional petticoats and undergarments is quite risqué.

In the 1960s designers also began to take an interest in men's clothes as a fashion rather than a uniform with very few variations.

It was time to rid men's suits of their nineteenth century styling and historic custom ... vents and slits are for horseback riding. Lapel buttonholes a

BIBA, London 1963–1975, reopened 1978, reopened 1994
Barbara Hulanicki, designer
Poland born 1936
Men's suit c. 1969
cotton corduroy, nylon
Presented by Rodney DeSoos 1995
1995.702a-c

BIBA, London 1963–1975, reopened 1978, reopened 1994
Barbara Hulanicki, designer
Poland born 1936
Granny dress c. 1968
cotton voile
Gift of Joanna Motion 1996   1996.120

LAURA ASHLEY, Carno, Wales
Laura Ashley, designer
Great Britain 1926–85
Dress and matching hat 1974
cotton, straw, imitation flower
Gift of the artist 1975   D3-1975

vestige of the dandy. We have buttons that do not button and pockets that have been empty for fifty years.[3]

Men's suits were traditionally made by tailors, but by the 1960s exclusive male boutiques stocked Nehru or Mao jackets in outrageous fabrics and corduroy flares, in standard sizes. The 'Peacock Revolution' was the term used to describe the major changes occurring in menswear at this time, styles for men that were colourful and flamboyant. Carnaby Street in London was the world centre. The Mod (short for modernist) sought out the new and different in clothes while the anti-Mod followers found the Art Nouveau and turn of the century looks, such as Biba.

'Today corduroy is the fabric of youth.'[4] Rediscovered for fashionable clothes, corduroy had in the past been used for working clothes. A woven fabric with a smooth back, its face is covered with short yarns known as the pile, divided by plain sections called ribs. The three-dimensional beauty of corduroy brings out the full bloom and impact of colour.

The Biba *Men's suit* (c. 1969) in an Edwardian style made of deep purple corduroy, has a tailored frock coat with exaggerated large lapels. It is single breasted, has three pockets, and is lined with purple satin. The matching pants have a lowered waist known as hipster, hip-huggers or low slung pants which feature the new zip fly to create a very tight or snug fit. The legs are slightly flared. This new form of trouser is an example of unisex fashions that could be worn by either sex.

B ba closed in 1975. An attempt to reopen in 1978 was not a success however the current revival of 1960s and 1970s styles has led to the label recommencing last year.

The Laura Ashley style was the total antithesis of the Swinging London scene. Ashley looked to Victorian times and the garb of 'milkmaids' for her inspiration and created an approach to dressing and living now known as 'country'. Her fashion influence and importance is often hugely underestimated.

Laura Ashley (Great Britain 1926–1985) began a small business in 1948 to try to develop patchwork as a home industry, and then began printing textiles by hand. In 1954 a small company was formed in London to handprint textiles, producing tea towels and nappery. By 1959 Ashley and her husband started designing basic garments such as gardening smocks sand aprons. In 1961 the company founded its factory at Carno in Wales where the cotton is b eached, washed, shrunk, dyed and batch printed. By 1968 the first retail shop had opened in Pelham S reet, South Kensington, London.

The trade magazine *American fabrics and fashions* in 1975 announced that:

Nineteenth century in feeling, Laura Ashley clothes possess precisely those qualities demanded today by a certain customer, who might once have been considered strange and 'artsy-craftsy' ... her clothes fit in with milk face washes, ethnic dress, and home-grown food.[5]

One might expect a twentieth-century girl to reject long or mid calf dresses, tight bodices, high necks and puffed sleeves, but they didn't. Ashley originally intended her garments to be casual wear for the house or garden but they were worn for all occasions including weddings and in the evening. Using only natural fabrics printed with traditional patterns such as flower sprigs or patchwork prints, Ashley designs rarely changed, staying cocooned in the past.

The *Dress and matching hat* (1974) is not a replica of Victorian costume but simply recreates elements of that era with its gathered sections, puffed s eeves and delicate patterning, reinforcing the image of a romantic idealised pastoral nymph. The sepia coloured design of small flowers is derived from a nineteenth-century hand-printed woodblock print and is transposed onto a natural cotton base. No attempt has been made in this garment to embrace modern dyes, print technology or contemporary styles, as if it is encapsulated in a time warp.

The styling of the dress involves various sections gathered and joined together to form a very full and expansive garment that would suit a range of figures. The matching hat, in brown trimmed with a flower, completes the natural country girl image, combining protection from the elements, a flirtatious accessory and a complete disregard for the present or future.

No future, punk couture

The 1950s revival shop Let it Rock opened in 1971 selling memorabilia and records. It was run by Malcolm McLaren (Great Britain born 1946) and Vivienne Westwood (Great Britain born 1941) at the back of Paradise Garage at 440 King's Road, London. In 1972, with a new name — Too Fast To Live Too Young To Die — it sold biker look clothes, and in 1974 became Sex a shop selling fetish/fantasy clothes.

Court shoes (c. 1977) are quite evil to look at. These high heeled black court shoes are decorated on the back with six silver blunt spikes, looking like some dangerous defence or device for inflicting pain.

McLaren and Westwood developed the concept that clothing could be subversive, and it was. In 1977 Seditionaries was born, perhaps ironically one of the most influential fashion phenomena of the late twentieth century. This series of clothes designed by Westwood and McLaren featured angst messages such as 'Destroy', and were ready ripped and soiled.

These garments were worn and popularised by the music group the Sex Pistols which McLaren managed, perhaps best remembered for their rendition in 1977 of 'God Save the Queen' — 'no future for you, no future for me'.

Punk represented a total revolt against style and society.

Punks wore clothes which were the sartorial equivalent of swear words, and they swore as they dressed ... Clothed in chaos.[6]

This type of clothing was not promoted in glossy fashion magazines, paraded on catwalks or sold in major department stores, yet its general effect on clothing styling was and still is phenomenal.

'Confrontation dressing' was a term used by Vivienne Westwood to describe clothing that rebelled against existing clothing norms and aroused feelings of anger in the viewers. These clothes were intentionally ill-fitting, ripped and torn, decorated with safety pins, swear words, confrontational messages and swastikas, using discarded clothing styles, and elements of kitsch; they challenged concepts of modernity, taste, and conventional ideas of prettiness and the success culture. Clothing now equated with rebellion.

This fashion revolt was next transformed into an upmarket form of decoration and dress. Perhaps one of the most literal translations in surface decoration of punk was created by Zandra Rhodes.

Zandra Rhodes (Great Britain born 1942), inspired by folk costumes and simple clothing forms, experimented and made a range of distinctive and unusual garments to enhance her original handprinted textile designs. She often called them Works of Art. Rhodes created a style of dress that was timeless, evoking the grandeur and imaginative detailing often found in fancy dress. Rhodes had graduated from London's Royal School of Art in 1966, having originally wanted to be a textile designer. She opened the Fulham Road clothes shop in 1968 in order to sell dresses made up from her own textile designs.

ZANDRA RHODES, London est. 1969
Zandra Rhodes, designer
Great Britain born 1942
Conceptual chic, top and skirt 1977–78
autumn/winter collection
rayon, glass beads, safety pins, imitation
pearls, ball chain
Gift of Robyn Beeche 1992   CT4A-B-1992

ZANDRA RHODES, London est. 1969
Zandra Rhodes, designer
Great Britain born 1942
Star check top, bubble skirt and sash 1977
silk, screenprint, sequins
Gift of Robyn Beeche 1992   CT2-1992A-C

The movie *Star Wars* was the catalyst for a series of Rhodes textile prints and costumes. Further exploring the idea of space and planets, she visited various museum collections and gathered postcards and slides. The Eduardo Paolozzi print she saw at the Victoria & Albert Museum in London gave her the inspiration to include a machinery component that transformed her space motifs, giving them mechanical style bends and simulated motion.[7]

Star Check top and bubble skirt (1977), in a soft beige chiffon, is screenprinted in an expansive pattern like a vision of the universe. The squiggly lines and dots representing star constellation patterns in blue, pink and cream are shooting off in all directions. The space theme is also repeated in the skirt, shaped like a sphere with an elasticised waist, and gathered again under the knees, perhaps simulating a planet ring. The skirt is printed with vertical rows of ringed planets and clusters of stars, the design Rhodes called 'Star Check'.

To enhance her textile designs Rhodes invented garment styles that required the minimum of cutting or shaping. This circular top, for instance, has short all-in-one sleeves and is gathered around the waist with elastic to form its basic shape. The neckline has a rouleau edge stitched at regular intervals in a zig-zag formation, weighted with an occasional sequin/jewel trim that pulls the garment against the body and allows the fabric to fall flat.

In her 1978 Punk Chic collection Rhodes challenged the norms of eveningwear and took inspiration from the Punk couture of Westwood and McLaren and the punk sub-culture of King's Road. Rhodes simulated various types of decorative effects to recreate the concept of a distressed garment that is ripped, inside out, or worn. Rhodes' idea was also influenced by Elsa Schiaparelli (Italy 1890–1973) with her 1938 Torn dress, an important iconic reference to surrealist design.

The *Conceptual chic, top and skirt* (1977–78) autumn/winter in black viscose rayon jersey is outlined in blue cotton overlocking stitching, along the seams and over the large random slashes. The slashes, joined by small gold safety pins threaded with glass beads, are studded with rhinestones, or ball link chains are draped across the cavities.

The label mentions that 'this garment has been / produced by hand in / Zandra Rhodes studio'. The surface decorations would be very time consuming and exacting, involving careful manipulatation of the cloth and correct positioning of the ornaments without severely damaging the cloth, and the original artistic rationale.

The holes are quite manicured and the process to create them complicated:

It proved quite difficult to make a 'beautiful tear' look like a tear. When the stitched edging was put on it totally lost its shape. So many different types of holes were cut and tried. Then we started decorating and pinning them.[8]

To stop the tears contorting the overall shape of the blouse and skirt, the safety pins, strategically positioned, structurally support the hole. The everyday safety pin was one of the major punk icons, a symbol of mockery against decorative embellishments (especially when threaded through the nose). Rhodes threaded her safety pins with fake jewels and decorated eveningwear with them.

The edges of the garment and holes are slightly curly, or 'lettuced' as Rhodes called the effect, created by stretching the fabric as it is oversewn.

Costume

Fashion is about constant change, a new style produced every season, and the production of new styles which depend on changes in the social, cultural and economic climate. Individual designers work on their own themes or philosophy of dress without radically changing the styling each season. A woman in the 'New Look' styling of the 1950s looked out-of-date immediately the mini dress was introduced. But now each season does not necessarily produce something newer or better, more progressive or modern. Instead, designers develop key features that recur or remain in their work.

If we look at just two of the major French ready-to-wear designers, Yves Saint Laurent and Karl Lagerfeld, both of whom won the International Wool Secretariat competition in 1954 and by the 1970s are still major instigators and promoters of certain styles of fashion, we can appraise the new character of fashion. It is clear that their approach and individual signatures have remained the same, and that this is their fashion's appeal and attraction.

YVES SAINT LAURENT, Paris est. 1962
Yves Saint Laurent, designer
France born 1936
Evening ensemble 1976–77
autumn/winter collection
comprising bolero, blouse and skirt
cotton, silk, jet
Purchased 1994   CT365A-C-1994

Yves Saint Laurent is perhaps the best known and most publicised designer of this century. The cynics would argue that perfume and well orchestrated marketing campaigns have secured this position, but they are wrong. Over the decades Saint Laurent has worked through a range of themes and styles, experimenting with clothes. He has sought inspiration from the major art movements and artists such as Mondrian and Matisse; he has looked at street sub-cultures, folk culture, history and much more. He has used clothing as a vehicle to express and interpret his diverse sources, and to create a comprehensive yet streamlined women's wardrobe.

Saint Laurent reinforces the idea that clothes are beautiful, appealing and draw attention to the wearer, due to the balance of function and aesthetic qualities. His garments make the wearer look and feel efficient, confident, and exude power.

In 1966 Saint Laurent launched a prêt-à-porter collection in Paris entitled 'Yves Saint Laurent Rive Gauche' (a name which referred to the traditional Left Bank location of small ready-to-wear boutiques).

In his ready-to-wear, Saint Laurent understood that a woman's wardrobe should be as comfortable as a man's. He saw no reason why women should have to throw away their clothes every season.[9]

For the next decades Saint Laurent based his collection on recurring themes and types of garments. His trademark designs are often underestimated today, because they are so widely copied and we are so accustomed to their elegant lines with only subtle variations. This is particularly true of his designs for daywear. Saint Laurent developed a day wardrobe based on the men's wardrobe with constant elements of a shirt, jacket, trousers (or skirt). This approach was to make dressing less complicated and permitted various basic garment types to be coordinated in many ways. This is now a standard concept of contemporary dress.

In 1966 he created his first tuxedo outfits called 'Le Smoking'. The theme of menswear recurs in his collections over and over again, as Saint Laurent reworks patterns of dressing and behaviour associated with dress styles and the notion of unisex fashions.

The original late-nineteenth-century dinner jacket or tuxedo had silk-faced lapels, a shawl collar and one button; it was an elegant garment. The tuxedo jacket is the shorter version and the hip length English equivalent, called a Smoking jacket, was made of velvet or a luxurious cloth, with a satin or velvet shawl collar, buttonless, tied with a sash and worn at home for informal entertaining.

By taking this standard garment for men and introducing it to womenswear, Saint Laurent strove to loosen the traditional barriers of certain types of clothing. *Le Smoking dress coat* (c. 1975) in black wool gabardine with velvet lapels and cuffs is based on the tuxedo jacket conventions but elongated to make a dress. Its stylistic origins are obvious but at the same time it has evolved into a new form.

Yves Saint Laurent is constantly inspired by other cultures, reinventing clothes in often extravagant and imaginative ways. Couture fashion was declared to be resurrected by Yves Saint Laurent with his Russian collection in 1976, focusing on the opulent and extravagant clothes that were synonymous with the couture industry and providing a dazzling return to fantasy style garments not seen since the 1950s. He transposed Russian costume and triggered a folklore wave which others followed, looking to other cultures for inspiration.

The fall/winter collection 1976–77 was hailed by the *International Herald Tribune* as 'the most dramatic and expensive show seen in Paris', containing what are still considered some of the most spectacular dresses ever designed. It was perceived as 'a revolutionary collection, which will change the course of world fashion'.[10]

The press christened the collection 'Ballets Russes'. However, the garments bore no resemblance to the ballet costumes of the famous Russian ballet company of Serge Diaghilev, except for their glitter and theatrical air. Their main reference to Russian culture is some basic styling associated with everyday peasant clothes.

The *Evening ensemble* (autumn/winter 1976–77) has a bolero jacket, peasant-style blouse and a bouffant yoke skirt, with attached petticoats. The vibrant red velvet bolero jacket is embroidered with black jet beads, and highlighted around the edges with a floral beaded design. This trimming perhaps simulates the Russian decorative device of soutache, the narrow flat decorative braid or peasant embroidery. The ensemble's black moiré full-length peasant skirt has a red velvet yoke encrusted with black jet beads and trimmed with black silk tassels. The fullness of the skirt is supported by an attached burgundy silk taffeta petticoat, with a flounce, over another black silk one, to shape the bulk of the garment. A gypsy-style blouse made from fine black chiffon woven with lamé pinstripes has a smouldering, glistening hue. It is lined with flesh-coloured chiffon.[11]

Yves Saint Laurent combines practicality with extravagance, delivering contemporary garments with restrained elegance or appealing to women's love of the decorative, with fabulous eveningwear. The concept now rarely changes.

Fashion artists, as previously noted, can look to history and render it new. The large vocabulary of surface decoration, applied work and detailed garments from the late nineteenth century involved exquisite hand sewing and long hours. Yet these antique gowns inspired Lagerfeld to simulate a range of ready-to-wear garments that echo these techniques and convey the sense of grandeur of that age.

Karl Lagerfeld (Germany born 1939) at the age of sixteen won an International Wool Secretariat competition and secured a position working for the Paris house of Balmain for several years. Subsequently he worked freelance for several ready-to-wear houses such as Krizia, Fendi and Chloé. By 1970 he was appointed chief designer at Chloé, retaining aristic control until 1983. His design vocabulary and history of ideas is immense.

Karl Lagerfeld's series of evening dresses for Chloé inspired by the delicate tea gowns of the Belle Epoque (known as lingerie dresses) were made from a confection of lace and fine fabrics. 'Women fought to have those dresses. I got calls from all over the world.'[12]

These tea gowns used materials and technical skills normally reserved for lingerie. Many people assume, incorrectly, that once ready-to-wear garments became an integral part of high fashion, intricate detailing disappeared except in couture

clothing. The allure of delicate fabrics, fussy detailing, ultra-feminine silhouettes, the secret garments of lingerie known only to a woman's closest acquaintances — these Lagerfeld made into a public garment.

In the *Tea gown* (c. 1978) he explores this idea by building up a palette of textures, layers and subtle decorative techniques. The cream silk tulle over-dress has a round collar and full sleeves, delicately embroidered with a design of green sprigs, and scalloped edges embroidered with pink and coral coloured flowers. This sheer garment, worn over a pale green cotton lawn slip with shoe-string straps, is also indicative of typical 'feminine' types of decoration.

Another example, *Tea gown* (1979), gives a more literal interpretation. The cream silk pieces with lace insertions create a patchwork effect or a complex textural jigsaw. Panels of silk running horizontally and vertically are linked by pieces of insertion lace.

The Chanel suit is perhaps one of the most recognised garments of the twentieth century. Gabrielle 'Coco' Chanel (France 1883–1971) reopened her house in 1954 and first designed the suit in jersey or a soft tweed material. It was usually collarless, braid trimmed, with a skirt falling just below the knee. The suit was worn with a coordinated silk blouse or blouson with a softly tied bow, accessorised with beige shoes with black toe caps, and a Breton hat. Imitation jewellery consisting of many strands of pearls or chains finished the outfit. The suit was a 1960s staple for those who could afford it, and appreciated the luxury of couture.

The *Suit* (c. 1965) comprising a cream wool jacket and matching skirt, is a perfect orchestration of form and fabrication. The main feature of the garment is the texture of the wool and the clean lines of its making. Its brass monogram buttons are the only obvious sign of embellishment. However, the most

CHANEL, Paris 1914–1939
re-opened 1954
Gabrielle 'Coco' Chanel, designer
France 1883–1971
Suit c. 1965
wool, brass buttons
Gift of Mavis Powell 1986   CT9-1986

CHLOE, Paris est. 1952
Karl Lagerfeld, chief designer 1964–84, 1992–
Germany born 1938, to France
Detail from *Tea gown* c.1979
silk, lace
Gift of Cynthia Staley 1996   1996.193.a-c

CHANEL, Paris est. 1914–39
re-opened 1954
Karl Lagerfeld, designer
Germany born 1939
Jenny Kee, textile designer
Australia born 1947
Suit 1983
comprising jacket, blouse, skirt and necklace
silk, metal
Gift of the House of Chanel through *Vogue*
Australia 1983   CT105-1983

interesting features are found with the couture finish. The interiors of the jacket and skirt are fully lined, hand stitched to the pure silk lining. Running along the lower back section of the lining of the jacket is a heavy gilt chain hand sewn to the top of the hem allowance and concealed by the fall of the lining. This device holds the jacket in place without riding forward with the wearer's movements.

When in 1983 Karl Lagerfeld was appointed chief designer at Chanel, he was inspired by the history of the house and its distinctive styling, and wanted to continue making some of Chanel's well known styles. Lagerfeld went about the deconstruction of the Chanel suit.

Printed form — cultural imprint

By using quirky and flamboyant contrasts of pattern and texture, and by altering the shape of the jacket and shortening the skirt, Lagerfeld updated and transformed the original Chanel suit.

The *Suit* (1983), made in black and white houndstooth check silk, is lined with black Opal Oz printed silk fabric, also in a matching blouson, designed by Jenny Kee (Australia born 1947). The jacket has, running along the inside lower hem, the faux fold chain edging to weight the jacket, as well as the signature interlocking C buttons. The new-style wrap-around skirt allows the Opal Oz lining to be seen as the wearer

moves, and creates a new dynamic force for the original Chanel concept. This ensemble represents a significant and successful fusion of Australian and international design.

In 1980 Jenny Kee had started working with Fabio Bellotti of Rainbow fabrics, in Milan, Italy, to utilise advanced methods of printing which were unavailable in Australia for her textile designs. Lagerfeld met Kee in Milan and expressed interest in what she was wearing, later contracting her to design exclusive opal-influenced fabrics for Chanel. Sixty-five garments in the Chanel prêt-à-porter collection of 1983 featured her fabrics in cotton, silk and organza, and some embroidered with sequins.

It's not often enough that we consider Australian fashion designers in the context of world fashion. Perhaps we still see our lifestyle and design considerations as too insular, or are wary of our enormous economic and market barriers, or perhaps we perceive our local designers as derivative. Yet if we look at Australian designers in a broader focus, we start to see some stimulating departures and imaginative approaches evolving from a very restrictive market environment. These include a form of unique, one-off garments, fabricated in a style reminiscent of couture and theatrical costuming techniques.

The work of Jenny Kee and Linda Jackson (Australia born 1950) sparked an interest in Australian fashion. It displayed adventurous styling and patterns that translated Australian culture and lifestyle into a unique form of clothing that evolved separately from world trends.

Kee studied fashion at East Sydney Technical College; Jackson studied at Emily McPherson College in Melbourne. After travelling extensively overseas and returning to Australia, they met in 1972 and collaborated to open a shop called Flamingo Park in the Strand Arcade, Sydney, to sell their own clothing and textile range. Flamingo Park closed in 1995. Their reliance on local icons and imagery for their inspiration and the dominance of the printed cloth against the construction of the garment is seen in the approach of Kee and Jackson.

From 1982 to 1991 Jackson ran her own design outlet, Bush Couture, at Bondi Junction, Sydney. Jackson's garments focus on her textile designs and the use of multi-layered clothing. Often basic clothing forms like ponchos or wraps could be worn around the wearer's body in various combinations, giving the garment individual style each time it

BUSH COUTURE, Sydney 1982–1991
Linda Jackson, designer
Australia born 1950
Artists of the Utopia Station, Northern Territory
Utopia costume 1982
comprising muumuu, poncho and four fabric lengths
silk satin, silk pongee, cotton; batik
Purchased 1992   CT32A-F-1992

was worn. *Utopia costume* (1982) comprises a muumuu, poncho and four fabric lengths which are wrapped and draped around the body. The batik fabrics were handpainted by various women artists from the Utopia Station in the Northern Territory. Jackson has carefully respected the textile designs and in most cases left the cloth uncut. The overall impact of the costume is fragmented, with only various sections of the clothing layers revealed. One becomes absorbed in the various fabrics and the primitive garment forms that make up this complex outfit, which evokes and respects the spirit of Aboriginal culture.

Notes

1   'What Saint Laurent has done, with his latest collection, is to remind us that fashion, in its radical form of couture, is costume ... it strikingly illustrates the degree of sophistication attained by fashion's analysis of history ... it's not nostalgia for the past, but for the eternal present which lies on the other side of the past'. Pierre Schneider, US *Vogue*, September 1976. Quoted in *Yves Saint Laurent Retrospective*, Art Gallery of NSW, Beaver Press, Sydney, 1987, p. 21.

2   Colin McDowell, *McDowell's directory of twentieth century fashion*, Muller, London, 1984, p. 86.

3   Ruben Torres, *Dress optional: the revolution in menswear*, Peter Owen, London, 1967, p. 94.

4   *American Fabrics*, number 85, Winter 1969–70, p. 53.

5   'Laura Ashley fabrics and clothing: harbinger for the late 70s', *American Fabrics*, number 103, 1975, p. 67.

6   Dick Hebdige, *Subculture the Meaning of Style*, Methuen & Co, New York, 1979, p. 7.

7   Zandra Rhodes & Anne Knight, *The art of Zandra Rhodes*, Jonathon Cape, London, 1984, p. 204.

8   ibid., p. 178.

9   Edmund White, 'The last emperor', *The Australian Magazine*, 19–20 November 1994, p. 23.

10 *Yves Saint Laurent Retrospective*, op. cit., p. 39.

11 This couture garment was made for the late Mrs Heard de Osborne, a Texan oil heiress married to a Spanish sherry merchant, who died in 1987. Her wardrobe of couture garments was auctioned at Christies South Kensington on 21 June 1994. The National Gallery of Victoria purchased several outfits and a group of hats.

12 'Inside Lagerfeld's mind', *Connoisseur*, September 1985, p. 107.

ISSEY MIYAKE, Tokyo est. 1971
Issey MIYAKE, designer
Japan born 1935
Bustier 1980–81
autumn/winter collection
fibreglass resin, felt
Purchased 1996   1996.102

Living Yesterday Tomorrow [1] — reworking clothing forms in the 1980s and 1990s

The 1980s was a period of high economic growth and spending: an environment that nurtured a boom in extravagant, labelled big name designer clothes, reminiscent of the couture boom of the 1950s. It produced clothing that reflected power and wealth, and lots of party clothes — luxury fashion. In this period designers also take on a demi-god or movie star status, as in the heyday of couture. Christian Lacroix (France born 1951) epitomises this period. After working for Patou from 1982 to 1986, with huge financial backing in 1987 he founded his own house. Lacroix is infamous for his extravagant garments built up from layers of embellishments and complex detailing. In the early days his work was often described by fashion journalists as unwearable, especially when he unleashed bouffant skirts with panniers in violently clashing colours. Lacroix believes that:

Fashion is like those Russian dolls: you open one up and another is inside, then another and another ... Through the seventies we see the forties, and the forties were inspired by the end of the nineteenth century.[2]

The recycling of fashion occurs again and again. Lacroix's combinations of style, colour and pattern are excessive, often creating a tension that makes viewers want to avert their eyes — but they are also extremely attractive and, dare I say, infectious.

As the fashion world experienced a return to the big names and their signatures of style, there was a movement towards reinterpretation of fashion concepts and a recognition of clothing's potential as a vehicle for change. Clothing norms were challenged as fashion artists developed new ways of making and thinking about clothing — by analysing and challenging its standard components, the way garments are formed, how the fabric is treated and even the psychological and physiological impact of such work. Artists literally took clothing apart and started again. Clothing was reconstructed and deconstructed: materials were slashed, spoiled and distressed, underwear worn as outerwear, poverty looks and regenerated looks abounded, and clothing was wrapped and worn in different manners. Designers created alternatives that were extreme and often shocked.

The fall of Babylon or fashion anarchy

In 1980 the London shop run by McLaren and Westwood was renamed World's End, after the bus stop location near the shop. This name also conjures up the Day of Judgement, the very last place you would wish to find a fashion boutique (or is that where one is really needed!).

The World's End label proudly boasts 'BORN IN ENGLAND' and depicts an arm, probably that of a buccaneer bearing a cutlass, a pirate image referring to McLaren and Westwood's basic design approach: 'to plunder the world of ideas' and create their own form of fashion rebellion.

The ability to shock is a major feature of Westwood and McLaren's work and their broader understanding of the concept of fashion, which includes its social implications, historical meanings and the vision that clothing is the synthesis of cultural ideas. 'For me fashion is to do with people's feelings about their culture and their lifestyle at a particular time,' said Malcolm McLaren.[3]

He perceived fashion as a means of expressing one's identity and as a vehicle for translating a variety of ideas. McLaren and Westwood 'plundered' the entire history of costume as they attempted to create clothing that was desirably different yet blended distinct cross-cultural influences in provocative and often primitive construction techniques. Their obsessive desire, create something new, lead them to revolt against the norm and experiment, to make clothing alternatives. The study of non-Western civilisations, in particular Aztec and Mexican cultures, inspired the Savage collection.

The *Dress rock and shoes* (spring/summer 1982), is made mainly from inexpensive fleecy cotton knit. The dress has uneven hems, and a bold pseudo-tribal pattern screenprinted in pink, grey and white. It is an unusual garment, its strange, quirky features sitting oddly against the body. The extra-wide long sleeves and too-tight cowl collar in a non-stretch fabric challenge its function of wear without ripping or destroying these parts. Sections of the dress use the sweat-shirt material reversed with the fluffy surface on the outside, like a fur. A message is emblazoned across the centre front of the dress: DRESS ROCK. The front of the dress is cut about 26cm shorter than the back, adding to the rough construction aesthetic and creating a primitive train.

The imitation rock shoes, in a Baby Jane style with three straps around the ankle in a dappled brown and beige, look like children's shoes.

The Savage collection cast aside traditional sewing techniques and neat garment forms, experimenting with ill fitting, oversized garments, often with exposed seams, in rough fabrics and using bizarre decorative effects.

This style inspired many kids to create their own original and shocking fashions, breaking down the hierarchical and elitist nature of fashion and introducing the notion of 'democratic fashion' or 'anti-status fashion'.

Westwood and McLaren exploited the expressive feature of costume to convey their views about politics, society, tradition and anarchy by challenging the traditional qualities of clothing and then using them as a billboard of communication. Their collaboration also successfully fused music and fashion with a release of a new fashion collection soon after the single 'B-BU-BUFFALO GALS'. This song was based on McLaren's concept of 'Found' sounds, music he would borrow from various sources and then remix as his own. In this case he took traditional square dancing commands, gave them a hip-hop beat, and added the scratching sounds of the gramophone needle moved manually backwards and forwards across the surface of the record.

WORLD'S END, London est. 1971
Vivienne Westwood, designer
Great Britain born 1941
Malcolm McLAREN, designer
Great Britain born 1946
Dress rock and shoes 1982
spring/summer collection
from the Savage collection
fleecy cotton, cotton, screenprint
Gift of Robyn Beeche 1992   CT7A-B-1992

*Four Buffalo Gals go round the outside
Round the outside Round the outside
Four Buffalo Gals go around the outside
And dossido your partners.*[4]

The *Buffalo Gal's outfit* (autumn/winter 1982–83) from the Hobo collection uses Airtex, a material normally used for underpants or singlets. This multi-layered garment combines a hooded long-sleeved top, two pairs of leggings and two skirts printed with the Buffalo Gal design.

The cotton overskirt is screen printed with images of cowgirls wearing broad-brimmed hats and full skirts, dancing at a Native American Indian dance ceremony. One of the Indians wears a case mask: in one hand he holds a rattle and in the other a dance flute. These figures are possibly inspired by the Kachina dances of the Hopi Indians. The underskirt of wool flannel is also printed with this pattern, yet it is almost indecipherable, like an aged cloth. The Hobo look followed McLaren's Robin Hood philosophy, to make the rich look poor so the poor would look rich. When displayed on the catwalk models square danced to Appalachian folk and tracking music and wore mud on their faces as make-up.

The first catwalk show in Paris in 1983 gave their designs huge international exposure and media coverage. In 1984 Vivienne Westwood and Malcolm McLaren's successful collaboration ended.

The next direction and phase of Westwood's solo career saw a change in her logo design, now embracing the past and the future — an orb encircled by a satellite: 'The traditional orb is what the Queen holds in her hand as a symbol of her power ... The satellite signifies the future'.[5]

Westwood has said: 'I'm obsessed with the quality of life, and you have a much better life if you wear impressive clothes.'[6] This statement encapsulates her unique faith in clothing design and an understanding of its cultural impact.

Westwood's complex ideas often involve multi-layers of meanings which extend to the presentation of the catwalk parades. For instance the 1990 Cut N'Slash collection can be interpreted in various ways. The Slashed garments may refer to the more recent punk slashes; or to the technique known as slashing or scissoring in use from the fifteenth to

WORLD'S END, London est. 1971
Vivienne Westwood, designer
Great Britain born 1941
Malcolm McLaren, designer
Great Britain born 1946
Details from *Buffalo gal's outfit* 1982–83
autumn/winter collection
cotton, wool, screenprint, leather
Gift of Robyn Beeche 1992   CT6A-F-1992

the seventeenth century (a historical, decorative technique which showed off and exposed the shirt or fabric underneath, creating a raised pattern); or it may refer to the ritualistic markings of the African tribesman's decorative scars. The amusing concept of nicks and slashing as extended to men's shaving is also cleverly referred to in the catwalk parade.

First of all I showed the tailoring and you didn't see any cuts in it; then I wanted to bring the cuts on and mix them in with it. So before I did I had Suzi come on with just a little pair of knickers with all these cuts on them and a plain white shirt over the top and some plain red satin high-heeled shoes, and a cut-throat razor. And then this bloke comes on with cuts in a vest and a pair of trousers all covered in cuts, and his face covered in shaving lather, and she started to shave him — just to let people know that we were going to start bringing in the cuts and slashes.[7]

VIVIENNE WESTWOOD, London est. 1985
Vivienne Westwood, designer
Great Britain born 1941
Male outfit 1990
comprising jacket, jeans and cod piece
from the Cut N'Slash collection
cotton, polyester, metal buttons
Purchased 1995   1995.15a-c

The *Male outfit* (1990) from the Cut N'Slash collection has a blue denim bomber-style jacket with long sleeves, embellished all over with vertical rows of slashed square cutouts, frayed and accentuated by vertical lines of denim rouleau edging. The jacket fastens down the front with a metal zipper. The white jeans are decorated dramatically with two rows of vertical slashes on each leg, with raw edges.

The frayed areas form an interesting surface decoration, exposing the wearer's skin and forming an alluring, soft, tactile surface.

Two gold metal buttons engraved with Westwood's logo are placed on the waist and one at the bottom of the fly to hold a cod piece in place. The red satin cod piece has a triple bow decoration. A cod piece, often padded and decorated, was a feature of menswear in the fifteenth and sixteenth century. Westwood's cod piece makes an amusing, vibrant and correct historical accessory on this slashed garment. The result is confrontational dress — people don't know where to look, or love it; they are attracted and repulsed at the same time.

The *Platform shoes* (1994) produce various reactions in viewers, especially the notion that they are impractical to wear and ridiculous. But these shoes can be worn. They have beautiful sculptural qualities and the sweep of red vinyl is

neatly seamed at the side of the toe so as not to mar the lines. The extreme height of the 16cm heel suggests countless historical references from the 1970s back to shoes from various cultures. Westwood's designs do present problems for the inexperienced wearer: recall the well-publicised fall of Naomi Campbell in the 1994 autumn/winter *prêt-à-porter* parade. Westwood herself wears shoes like this and recommends wedges of tissue between each toe and rubber ballet toe caps for comfort.[8]

Westwood's influence as a catalyst for other fashion designers and the general market place is astounding. Her clothing forms and ideas, from rubber to bras on the outside, rips, oversized clothing and exposed construction details are the precursors of the 'New Dressing' Japanese clothing style in the 1980s and later the Belgian deconstructionist aesthetic of the 1990s.

Gender bender

Inspired by the London street scene Jean Paul Gaultier (France born 1952) brought to fashion crazy juxtapositions of patterns, colour, textures and kitsch decorations to challenge the taste boundaries of establishment clothing. Having trained at the traditional French couture houses of Cardin and Patou, in 1976 he established a ready-to-wear label based in Paris.

JEAN PAUL GAULTIER, Paris est. 1976
Jean Paul Gaultier, designer
France born 1952
Detail from *Male outfit* 1989
comprising cardigan and leggings
spring/summer collection
cotton, acetate, viscose, lycra, elastane
Purchased 1995   1995.12a-b

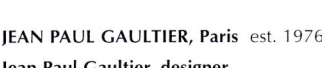

On the intellectual level he is truly a post-modernist artist, working by setting one concept against another, placing things in ironic ofter hilarious quotes.[9]

Gaultier's clothing designs revolt against the conventional mixtures of materials, style and form. His clothing forms invite and incite extreme reactions such as corsets and conical bras.

Gaultier released his first menswear collection, entitled 'Object-Man', in 1984 and experimented with the clichéd images of man and woman. He introduced for men elements of clothing associated with womenswear — not just skirts and leggings but also decorative elements such as embroidery and bows, to create 'pretty' menswear. Like Yves Saint Laurent, Gaultier examined the traditional patterns of sexual demarcation in clothing. Certain materials, styles of embellishments and the most outrageous and extravagant garments were reserved for women. In the autumn/winter 1985 collection Gaultier introduced skirts for men, a convenient alternative to trousers. It was viewed as a novelty and an attempt to shock the fashion world, and entered into taboo-breaking ground. Gaultier sold only 3000 men's skirts worldwide and they certainly didn't become a standard menswear option.[10] There seemed no logical reason for this other than the market. Men simply don't like wearing skirts.

Male outfit (spring/summer 1989) is a body hugging combination. The cardigan is decorated like an exquisite oriental robe. The pale blue machine-knitted front panels are richly embroidered with a Chinese-style pattern of flowers and butterflies. The sleeves are in a jacquard knit in a variegated pattern in shades of mustard and yellow. The back features an ornate jacquard pattern with minute squares and circles in shades of blue, mustards and red. The outfit is worn with a pair of black stretch leggings and silver spats over the shoes.

Forming a second skin

Kenzo Takada (born 1940) can perhaps be credited with leading the invasion of Western fashion styling by Japanese designers. Although his designs were based on the traditional mode of European fashion, his layering of colour, pattern and texture in the 1970s was the precursor to the innovative Japanese styles.

In the 1980s a major force in the direction of world fashion was the recognition of Japanese designers such as Issey Miyake and Rei Kawakubo (Japan born 1942) of Comme des Garçons working in alternative manners, materials and construction to traditional Western clothing types.

Rei Kawakubo in 1981 showed her collection for the first time in the ready-to-wear parades in Paris. Her early collections, with asymmetrical, over-sized garments and unorthodox use of holes and slashes stunned the fashion establishment. Kawakubo's clothing designs are severe yet functional; she creates new fabrics, and clothing shapes. Each collection is quite different, focusing

on a new making process or aesthetic. Perhaps her use of texture is an overriding feature. Like a sculptor Kawakubo manipulates cloth in extraordinary ways, by shrinking, stretching, overdyeing or bleaching. The garments often feature irregular components; for example one sleeve can be entirely different from the other.

The *'Deconstructivist' jacket, singlet top and crop top* (spring/summer 1992) exposes the construction stages of a tailored jacket with tacking threads, and the long sleeves are unattached under the arms, revealing an incomplete stage of the making process. The satin fabric in an orange, black, red and yellow geometric satin is stonewashed, resulting

ISSEY MIYAKE, Tokyo est. 1971
Issey Miyake, designer
Japan born 1935
Bustier 1980–81
autumn/winter collection
fibreglass resin, felt
Purchased 1996   1996.102

in an irregular faded and distressed appearance. The front and back feature asymmetrical elongated fins of fabric created by machine sewing and manipulating the loose folds of fabric to form three-dimensional decorations. The raw edges of cotton on the tops are sealed with a glue technique.

Issey Miyake (Japan born 1938) investigates new interpretations of clothing by focusing on the cloth and its relationship to the body. Miyake trained in Paris at the Chambre Syndicale de la Couture Parisienne, later working in Paris for the houses

Miyake concentrates on two significant themes: he explores the countless and exciting possibilities of new materials and he is committed to developing garments that are functional and comfortable for everyday life. His garments also work on a third level, as sculptural objects to be admired apart from a body form. He is perhaps one of the few designers to have created a garment that can work visually and structurally away from a body.

In 1980 Miyake participated in the organisation of the exhibition *Evolution of Fashion: 1835-1895* at

ISSEY MIYAKE, Tokyo est. 1971
Issey Miyake, designer
Japan born 1935
Reversible bomber jacket 1992
spring/summer collection
polyester
Purchased 1995   1995.14

of Laroche and Givenchy and in New York for Geoffrey Beene. Miyake was in Paris during the student revolt of May 1968. Afterwards, his attitude to fashion changed and he was inspired to look to traditional styles of Japanese costume to find an alternative fashion form catering to the needs of modern life. His first collection in 1971 was shown in Tokyo and New York. In 1973 he started participating at the prêt-à-porter catwalk parades in Paris. Miyake moved away from the traditional Western process of cutting up pieces of fabric, for tailoring or manipulating and sewing together fabric. He incorporates the techniques of ancient Japanese costume, using fabric wrapping, draping and layering it around the body to shape clothing.

the National Museum of Modern Art, Kyoto. The corsets and underwear in this display made Miyake observe 'the relationship between the body and the clothes and the space between them'.[11] This insight lead to the development of a series of garments known as Bodyworks.

The *Bustier* (1980–81) consists of a solid moulded shape made of a lustrous red polymer resin which hugs the wearer's body by imitating the front of a female torso. The form extends from the waist to hip to simulate a bodice ruffle. The inside surface is completely lined with a black synthetic velvet felting adhered to the resin, creating a comfortable soft barrier against the skin.

ISSEY MIYAKE, Tokyo est. 1971
Issey Miyake, designer
Japan born 1935
Dress 1994
spring/summer collection
from the Flying saucer collection
polyester, pleated and heat set
Purchased 1995   1995.781

Like armour, the bustier is a protective garment and also an alluring form representing an ideal woman's torso.

In the spring/summer 1989 collection Miyake showed his first pleated garments and now each season he reworks the pleat theme with great virtuosity. For Miyake:

Pleats move and change form with the wearer's body movements. As the pleats move they change colours, giving an optical illusion like a kaleidoscope ... Pleats contain endless fascination for me and also inspire a multitude of images.[12]

Miyake's pleated garments rely on the complex pleated surface decoration to give the clothing geometric pattern and shape without detailed cutting or sewing. Unlike the pleated robes from antiquity softly hanging in loose folds from the shoulders, or the early twentieth century crimped and irregular finely handpleated tea gowns by Mariano Fortuny, Miyake's pleats are hard edged, dynamic lines formed in various directions.

Using the heat set pleating technique with great inventiveness and also utilising the very latest in textile technology, Miyake first creates the basic garment shape and then pleats it. This approach is described by the costume curator Richard Martin as a form of cubism:

Miyake has used pleating as an abstract construction in the same manner of cubes, cones and constituents of cubist form. If the forms fall to reiterate the body's symmetry of joinings, they

BODYMAP, London est. 1982
Stevie Stewart, designer
Great Britain born 1958
David Holah, designer
Great Britain born 1958
Hilde Smith, textile designer
Great Britain born 1960
*Sun and Moon coat, ball dress, Cosmic
nature hat and platform shoes* 1986
spring/summer collection
nylon, cotton, screenprint, felt, leather
Purchased 1986   CT11A–D-1986

*may seem to resemble a figure, but more often
they create their own alternative structure, a planar
puzzle that defies the body, denying its references
in favour of planes as solid forms exchanging
space with the void that surrounds the form'.13*

The *Reversible bomber jacket* (spring/summer
1992) displays one of Miyake's complex pleating
translations. The jacket is made up of various
sections sewn together like a simple patchwork.
However, one side is made with horizontal bands
of polyester satin in bright yellow, green, orange
and black finely pleated sections. A green and red
zipper down the centre front allows the reversible
garment to be worn in two ways. The other side of
the jacket has vertical bands of polyester chiffon, in
black, fluoro green, red, grey and blue, also finely
pleated. When the chiffon side is worn on the
outside the satin bands show through, creating
an illusion of coloured squares.

The *Dress* (spring /summer 1994) from the
Flying saucer collection is a costume of ingenious
construction that can be an exquisite assemblage
of three pleated discs that sit neatly on a shelf or
can stretch out like an open fan and evolve to
form a shimmering dress of pleats. The dress is
striking, combining a series of concertina folds
and heat-set seams in vertical pleats. The stark
black sleeves against the palest green body produce
an eccentric rigid pattern that changes shape as
the wearer moves. The hard edges of the horizontal
folds create a series of shapes reminiscent of flying
saucer space craft, hovering over one another.

Clothes speak

Clothes act as billboards for messages and images
about our world, events, thoughts and crazy ideas.
David Holah (Great Britain born 1958) and Stevie
Stewart (Great Britain born 1958) formed BodyMap
in September 1982 after they both graduated from
the Middlesex Polytechnic with honours.

Their name derived from an artwork by the Italian
artist Enrico Job, who photographed every part of
his body and cut up the bits and rejoined them to
create a 3-D form on a flat plane. This seemed to
reinforce the concept of BodyMap's own inventive
form of pattern making.

BodyMap produced imaginative and thought
provoking collections featuring industrial or
sportswear materials such as stretch knit and
jersey, different textures and distinctive prints
based around a quirky theme such as 'A Cat in

the Hat takes a Rumble with a Techno Fish'. The
collections used bad taste or kitsch elements that
reinforced the assumption that fashion could be
outrageous and designed to amuse.

*Sun and Moon coat, ball dress, Cosmic nature hat
and platform shoes* (1986), from the BodyMap, Is
a comet a star ... a moon, ... a sun ... aura racoon?
spring/summer collection, applies Spinnaker nylon,
more normally used for shower curtain material
or industrial purposes, as the base cloth.

The black and white long tent dress tagged with
symbols of the Sun and Moon has a matching coat
decorated with racoons, and various astrological
symbols heralded the 1986 arrival of Halley's
Comet. The outfit was worn with a black bowler
hat trimmed with matching fabric.

Unfortunately the nature of this collection did
not attract many buyers and BodyMap closed
temporarily, reopening in the 1990s.

The English designer Katharine Hamnett (Great Britain born 1948) consciously uses clothes as a medium for comment on topical events and political messages and a way for people to stand up for particular causes by choosing to wear these items and raise people's consciousness. Part of her mainstream fashion line includes a series of 'Slogan' T-shirts, the profits from the sale of which go to a charity fighting child abuse. Hamnett has emblazoned T-shirts with messages such as 'Stop Acid Rain', 'Preserve the Rainforests' and 'Stay Alive in 85'.

Stay Alive in 85, T-shirt (spring/summer 1985) in bright red silk has the slogan for the anti-heroin campaign in England emblazoned in bold black print across its front.

Independent fashion designers — Antipodean design

In 1983 the Fashion Design Council (FDC) of Australia was formed in Melbourne:

committed to the development of the art of fashion design, to the individualistic, the idiosyncratic, the experimental, the new and provocative, both in its

SARA THORN, Melbourne est. 1983–85
ABYSS, Melbourne est. 1985–1992
Sara Thorn, designer
Australia born 1961
Bruce Slorach, designer
Australia born 1961
Men's jacket and kilt 1985
cotton, screenprint, metal buttons
Gift of the National Gallery Women's
Association 1995   1995. 765a-b

The FDC closed in 1993 after funding difficulties. However during the decade of its existence it boosted the Australian fashion industry by giving designers who ran small production lines an opportunity to expose their work on a larger scale. Morrissey & Edmiston, Tamasine Dale, Stephen Davies, Sara Thorn, Bruce Slorach and Jenny Bannister are among the inaugural designers.

Sara Thorn and Bruce Slorach created garments for men and women using inventive textiles they designed themselves with themes as diverse and perverse as flying phalluses, Robocops, smiley William Morris angels and Moderno tourists. Thorn (Australia born 1958) studied fashion and textile design at East Sydney Technical School and Sydney College of the Arts from 1980 to 1983. Slorach (Australia born 1958) studied art at Prahran College in 1979 and painting and printmaking at the Victorian College of the Arts. In 1983 they founded a fashion and textile business in Melbourne. It was originally known as the Sara Thorn label, later adopting the names Shrubbery, Abyss, and finally Galaxy.

Designing in Australia posed various problems in the local market place, which seemed to prefer European labels: 'Working in Australia, one is in almost total isolation from the international fashion brain — we see them but they don't see us'.[15] By making and designing their own clothes and textiles and using local manufacturers, Thorn and Slorach retained total control over the entire design concept. Their garments are explosive, literally sprayed with elements of popular culture and exude personality, fun and adventure. They created casual clothing styles for night clubbing or streetwear. The textile is their visual means of communicating ideas: 'in a way it's like having a dialogue with the customer, influencing them by what they wear. Commenting and creating culture' (artist's statement).

The *Men's jacket and kilt* (1985) in black cotton is hand silk screen printed in red and blue with a complex pattern comprising a 'Greek boarder (sic)' design, Napoleonic bees, winged boots and robot faces. Lined with tartan, the costume alludes to the Scottish kilts worn by men, made with knife pleats. Just as each Highland clan has a unique pattern, these motifs are distinctive to the Galaxy clan and their meaning often is known only to the designer.

Sequenced bra top and hot pants (1989) has a padded bra decorated overall with embroidery of glass beads and sequins and trimmed along the

wearable and unwearable form. It is critical of and sees itself separate to the conventions of mainstream and commercial fashion, the European tradition, the stranglehold of fashion houses.14

The FDC, formed with financial assistance from the Victorian State government, aimed to promote and encourage the independent Australian fashion design scene through (now considered quite legendary) fashion parades, exhibitions, media and as a retail, advisory and resource centre.

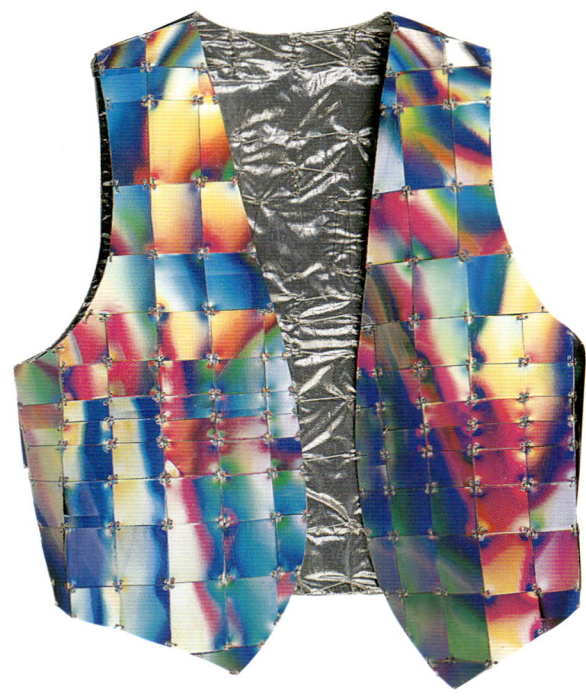

edges with gold-coloured braid. Each bra cup features an eye and beaded fringing runs along the bottom edge.

The matching hipster shorts feature an eye on each hip and flames flickering up from the hem. This is a garment designed for night clubbing and dancing the night away. Thorn and Slorach's work gained enormous exposure through music and television identities such as the Beastie Boys, Kylie Minogue, Cyndi Lauper and Alice Cooper wearing their garments.

By 1992 Thorn and Slorach founded a new label called Funkessentials, later known as the Konka brand, to broaden their commercial base. In 1995 their business closed.

Peter Tully (Peter Tutangi 1947–1992) inspired a genre in Australian clothing design using found objects and industrial, quirky materials that has influenced garments in movies such as *Mad Max* and *Priscilla Queen of the Desert*. Tully's clothes were categorised as Art clothes, a term coined after the exhibition Jane de Teliga curated at the Art Gallery of New South Wales in December 1980. As a term 'Art clothes' gives the impression that the garments are impractical, outrageous yet highly desirable. Tully called his own garments Urban Tribalwear.

The *Early flight attendant's vest* (1990) is a pulsating patchwork of retrospectra graphic plastic, the tagged centre back having a holographic image of an eye. Exhibited at the Barry Stern Galleries in Sydney

in the exhibition *Treasures of the Last Future* 1990, it was a response to the major retrospective exhibitions such as *Civilization: Ancient Treasures from the British Museum* (National Gallery of Australia and the Museum of Victoria 1990) and *The Age of Sultan Suleiman the Magnificent* (Art Gallery of New South Wales and National Gallery of Victoria, 1990).

A garment created from a fictitious world, rediscovered through excavations, was Tully's theme. However, with its shimmering surface and muse about the unknown, this garment inspires us to look to the future. The eye is watching our every move.

The concept of urban tribalism is also reflected in the work of the young Australian artist Sarah

Peter TULLY

Australia 1947–1992
Early flight attendant's vest 1990
lamé, metallic thread, retrospectra
graphic plastic
Purchased from Admission Funds 1991
CT1-1991

Harmarnee (Great Britain, Australia born 1970). She 'wanted to create something that made the body desirable, she sees food as an object of desire and cutlery a metaphor of that desire'.[16] The *Breastplate* (1994) is made up of eighteen small forks and eighteen small knives cast from a Victorian doll's cutlery set, in sterling silver, pieced together with plastic tubes and beads. Inspired by the breastplates of the Sioux Indians, this piece offers protection as a form of armour, a whimsical reflection of childhood or an allusion to the body as food.

Deconstruction inside outside

In the 1980s the Japanese designers introduced new ways of interpreting clothing forms and decorative devices: in the 1990s the Belgian designers contributed with a form of clothing known as deconstruction. The Antwerp Six, comprising Dirk Van Saen, Dries Van Noten, Walter Van Beirendonck, Anne Demeulemeester, Marina Yee and Dirk Bikkembergs, began exhibiting their clothing collectively at London Fashion

Sarah HARMARNEE

Australia born 1970
Breastplate 1994
sterling silver, leather, plastic tubing and beads
Purchased 1994   CT430-1994

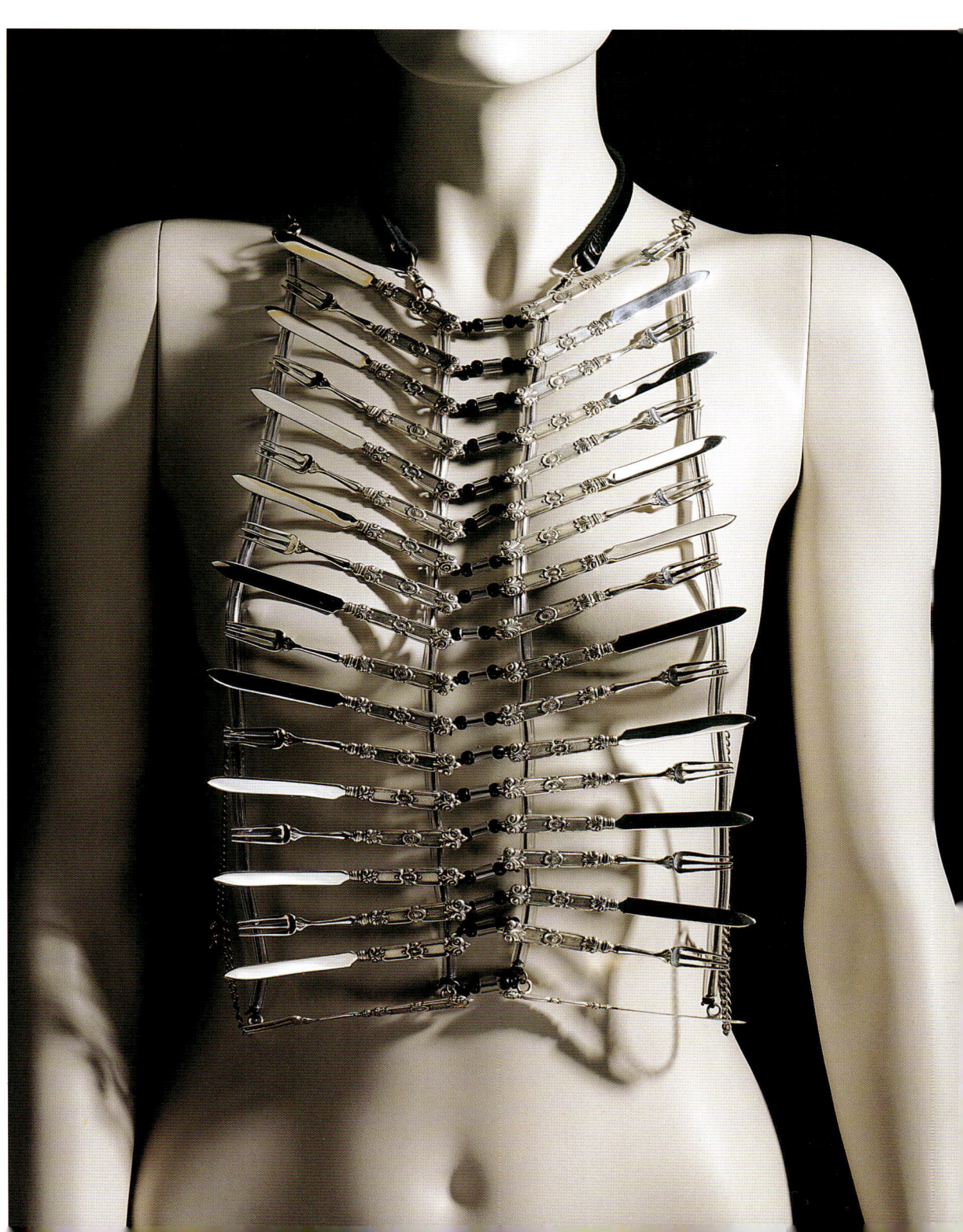

Week in 1988. This was of great importance for Flemish fashion: for the first time since the sixteenth century, when its lace and collars were world renowned, Belgium came to be acknowledged as a significant fashion centre.

Dirk Bikkembergs (Germany born 1959) studied fashion at the Antwerp Art Academy. Specialising in menswear, in 1985 he won the Golden Spindle award, an annual contest organised by the Institute for Belgian Textile and Ready-to-wear, encouraging collaboration between manufacturers and designers. It was this event that triggered the collaboration between Bikkembergs and the cobblers Rik and Jeff Verelst from Lier, and an important partnership was formed. Describing his shoe designs, Bikkembergs said:

They were like stones, when the industry was still overrun with paper-thin — Italian shoes. They were the first heavy looking shoes.[17]

Loafers (1996) have a wedge wooden platform sole, stepped and stacked in five layers. The front of the upper has an extended tap Velcroed to the throat, and large bullnose toes. Roughly overpainted in red, the grain of the wood and leather shows through. The shoe combines elements of a traditional loafer with a carved wooden clog and the heaviness of a work boot.

Martin Margiela (Belgium born 1957) graduated from the fashion course at the Royal Academy of Fine Arts in Antwerp. From 1983 to 1987 he worked as a design assistant to Jean Paul Gaultier in Paris.

In 1989 he presented his first collection. Margiela refuses to give interviews or do photo sessions, as he believes the time for designers to be superstars is over, and natural shyness rather than pretension is the reason he takes this stance. The notion of deconstruction translated into clothing implies that garments are taken apart and we either witness part of this process or the concept of using a found garment in another form. The analysis of a garment from an earlier period of dress and connecting the new garment to its predecessor implies a deconstructionist approach.

Margiela recreates old garments and their interiors, transposing the construction details of the garment to the outside to form part of its decoration. People need to learn about and appreciate the aesthetics of a garment created with the inside on the outside. There is a starkness and beauty about these

garments. It is interesting that people always ask us about the interiors of clothes and suddenly we are exposed to an aspect of clothing we normally do not see.

Dress, overdress and vest (autumn/winter 1992–93) comprises a series of garments inspired and recreated from old clothes. The dress is a reproduction of a German dress lining from the 1950s in a gold-coloured lining fabric. It displays all the exposed seams, overlocking, zipper and even the facing around the neck. The inside bears a large cotton label explaining the garment's stylistic origin: REPRODUCTION OF A SERIES / OF GARMENT INTERIORS / Dress lining. Germany / 1950s. Worn over this is a see-through crinkled

MARTIN MARGIELA, Paris est. 1989
Martin Margiela, designer
Belgium born 1957, to France 1985
Bustier/wrap 1995
spring/summer collection
cotton, viscose rayon, leather, elastic
Gift of Janet Purves 1996   1996.562.c

▶

DIRK BIKKEMBERGS, Antwerp est. 1987
Dirk Bikkembergs, designer
Germany born 1959
Loafer 1996
leather, wood, paint
Purchased 1996   1996.185.a-b

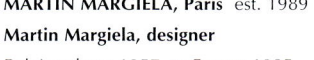

MARTIN MARGIELA, Paris est. 1989
Martin Margiela, designer
Belgium born 1957, to France 1985
Dress, overdress and vest 1992–93
autumn/winter collection
viscose rayon, polyester organza, hair, cotton
cord, metal
Gift of Janet Purves 1996   1996.558.a-d

MARTIN MARGIELA, Paris est. 1989
Martin Margiela, designer
Belgium born 1957, to France 1985
Singlet, skirt, bustier/wrap and choker 1995
spring/summer collection
cotton, viscose rayon, leather, elastic
Gift of Janet Purves 1996   1996.562.a-d

dress described on its inner label as: Transparent over-dress / Belgium. 1920s. Margiela does not use his name on the garments; instead, he offers careful descriptive titles that refer to the garment's history and immediately place the garment in context.

The vest is made with two layers of fabric sewn together but with no finished edges so the garment continues to fray. Also exposed on the edge is the care label showing size, care and fabric details. Around the neck a thong with a lock of hair is worn.

In *Singlet, skirt, bustier/wrap and choker* (spring/summer 1995) Margiela builds up in layers

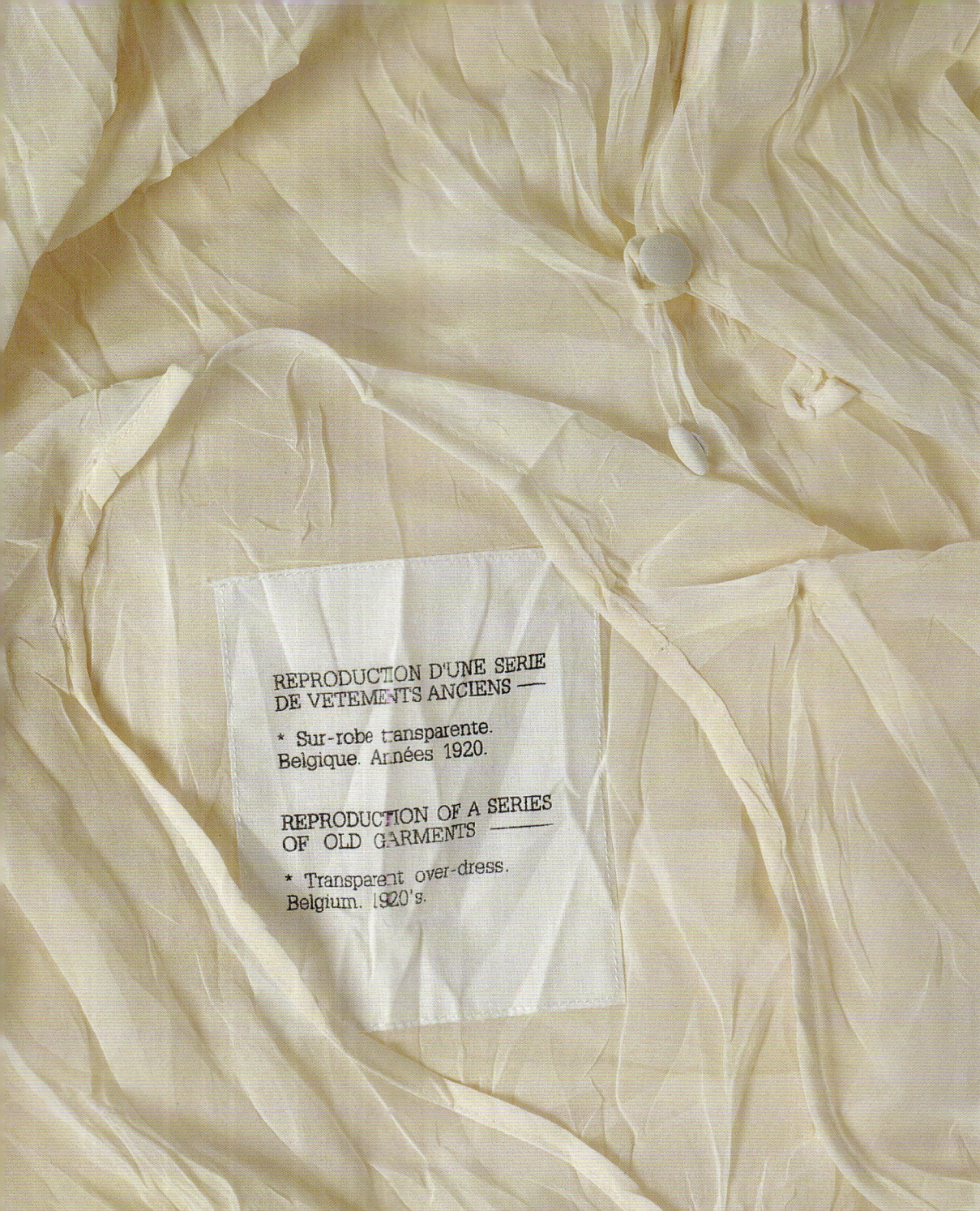

MARTIN MARGIELA, Paris est. 1989
Martin Margiela, designer
Belgium born 1957, to France 1985
Detail from *Dress, overdress and vest*
1992–93
autumn/winter collection
viscose rayon, polyester organza, hair, cotton
cord, metal
Gift of Janet Purves 1996   1996.558.b

an unusual arrangement of garments. One of the most interesting interpretations is the shirt that is worn in a new manner. Instead of the wearer placing her arms through the sleeves, the garment is worn with the buttons at the back and the sleeves wrapped around the torso. The garment is simply modified by sewing a piece of cotton tape on the end of each sleeve so it can tie together and a piece of elastic joined at each edge of the neck.

This outfit is from a series of garments known as: HAND-MADE PRODUCTION / (PRODUCTION ARTISANALE) Article made by hand from new or used clothing, objects and accessories. Production of these clothes is labour intensive.

Notes

1   'We live in a world with no particular cultural point of view. Living Yesterday Tomorrow is the preoccupation of the world's inhabitants who are trying desperately to get back to where there was such a point of view'. Malcolm McLaren interviewed by Michael Herrmann 1996, *Living Yesterday, Tomorrow*, 1996 Australian lecture programme.

2   Diane Rafferty, 'Christian Lacroix — the art of sensuality', *Connoisseur*, London, June, 1989, p. 78.

3   McLaren, interview, op. cit.

4   'B-BU-BUFFALO GALS' by McLaren, Dudley and Horn, 1982.

5   Caryn Franklin, 'Rule Britannia', Interview with Vivienne Westwood, *i-D*, The Metropolitan issue, No. 45, London, 1987, p. 75.

6   Vivienne Westwood, 'Royal flush', *i-D*, The Holiday issue, No. 50, London, 1987, p. 57.

7   Juliet Ash, 'Philosophy on the catwalk: the making and wearing of Vivienne Westwood's clothes', *Chic Thrills*, Pandora Press, London, 1992, p. 172.

8   Shane Watson, Designer of the decade, *Elle*, Emap Elan, London, November 1995, p. 58.

9   Sarah Mower, 'Gaultier', *Arena*, London, July/August 1987, p. 85.

10   ibid.

11   *Issey Miyake: Ten Sen Men*, Hiroshima City Museum of Contemporary Art, Hiroshima, 1990, p. 90.

12   Mark Holburn, *Issey Miyake*, Taschen, Germany, 1995, p. 82.

13   Richard Martin, 'The cubism of Issey Miyake, 1989–1990', *Textile & Text*, vol. 12, number 4, Fashion Institute of Technology, New York, 1990, p. 8.

14   Colin Wood, 'The Fashion Design Council of Australia', *Design World*, No. 10, 1986, p. 21.

15   Kayt Jones, 'The Outsiders', The High Spirits issue, *i-D*, No. 78, March 1990, p. 57.

16   Sarah Harmarnee 1995 Australian PR release.

17   Brigid Grauman, 'Dirk Bikkembergs', *The Face*, Nick Logan, London, July/August 1988, p. 75.

Kiss the future [1]

The way clothes are made has altered in the last forty years through the development and refinement of synthetic fabrics, advances in the general cleaning and maintenance of garments, the use of complete sewing machine construction and finish, the development of alternative technologies such as heat setting processes and computer design.

Fashion artists can use a garment as a vehicle for confrontational ideas, as a symbol of extravagance, a practical, comfortable form of attire, a canvas expressing colour, a sculptural form, a psychological attraction, an experimental structure or a means of amusement. Of course some clothes encompass many of these elements. Modern fashion now eclectically plunders from the past and has a large vocabulary of ideas to consult and absorb. There are no longer rules of dress to impose taste on the designer or wearer.

During the 1960s designers created space age looks worked with radical fabrics and fantasised about what people would wear in the year 2001. Now that date is only five years away. If fashion design still relies to a large extent on its saleability, does this inhibit clothing forms from evolving further and prohibit designers from taking risks? Commercial considerations control or inhibit the more extreme interpretations. That is where the significance of the small independent designer lies. Independent designers can contribute by providing alternatives and altering people's

W. & L.T. Paris est. 1994
Walter Van Beirendonck, designer
Belgium
Detail from *T-shirt* 1994–95
autumn/winter collection
polyamide nylon, PVC plastic, cotton
Purchased 1996   1996.201.a

perception of fashion. Do we still need seasonal collections — autumn/winter, spring/summer — or the traditional eveningwear and daywear styles or separate male and female collections? Has fashion evolved very far? Perhaps we are not encouraging fashion to advance any further?

The French designer Jean Paul Gaultier in 1982 suggested that fashions for the year 2001 would be 'Spray on' and 'dispose of it at the end of the day ... seamless without openings', 'the "second skin" body suit will serve as a basic uniform.'[2] This garment would require no sewing machine construction, pattern making or cutting of cloth and need absolutely no cleaning. (Can you imagine preserving that type of garment in a museum collection?)

Fashion no longer seems to cause a major change or improvement in our lifestyle, though perhaps it will again. We wait patiently for the dress you never have to clean or a garment that is cool in summer and warm in winter, or a bodysuit that is sprayed on from a pressure pack.

As fashion mixes art and commerce, the economy has a major impact on its direction. We are currently experiencing a return to conservatism, designers have become locked into retail demand. Are we due for another period like the 1960s to purge the old fashion ideas and look to the future? Or is fashion dead, and costume now the only relevant title to describe our clothing forms?

While we look to the future these are the challenges for the fashion artists of the twenty-first century.

Couture to chaos has attempted to expose its audience to a range of fashion artists and clothing forms, and ambitiously attempted to guide you through ways of looking at and interpreting fashion. Due to lack of space and the ongoing sourcing of works for this display it was not possible to include all artists represented in the exhibition in the catalogue and I apologise for this.

However, this publication is intended as a springboard and a starting point for other intensive surveys.

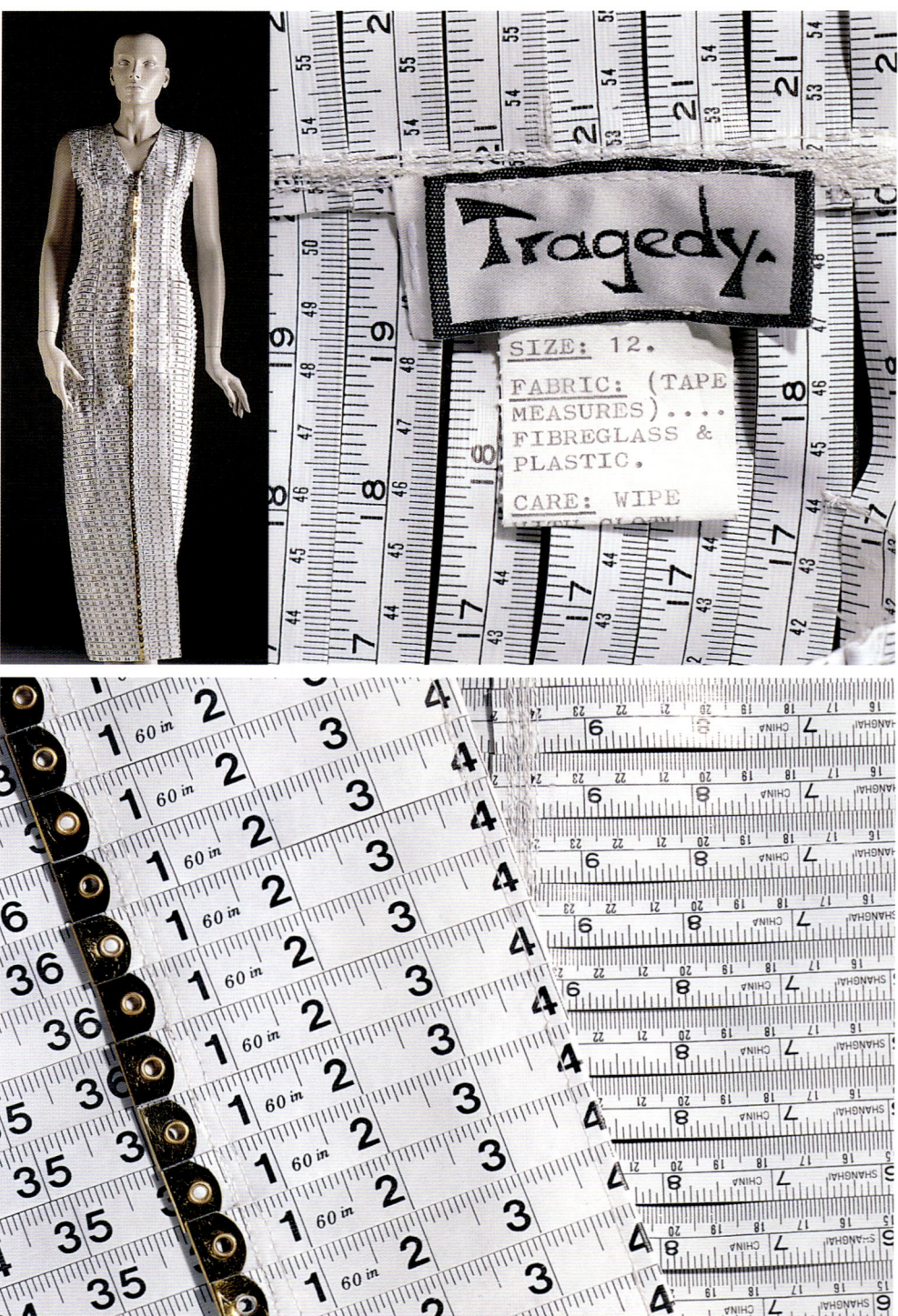

Notes

1   'Kiss the future — we need to believe that the future's bright. We need to be positive.' Walter Van Beirendonck of W. & L.T. (Wild and Lethal Trash), quoted in 'Fashion: little earth', *The Face*, No. 89, February 1996.

2   Lucille Khornak, *Fashion 2001*, Viking Press, New York, 1982, p. 62.

TRAGEDY, Melbourne est. 1993
Steven Bruton, designer
Australia born 1971
Tape measure dress 1994
tape measures, zipper
Purchased 1994   CT443-1994

Select bibliography

Aragno, Bonizza Giordani (ed.), *Moda Italia: creativity and technology in the Italian fashion system*, Editoriale Domus, Milan, 1988.

Ash, Juliet & Wilson, Elizabeth (eds), *Chic thrills*, Pandora Press, London, 1992.

Bennett-England, Rodney, *Dress optional — the revolution in menswear*, Peter Owen, London, 1967.

Chenoune, Farid, *A history of men's fashion*, Flammarion, Paris, 1993.

Coleridge, Nicholas, *The fashion conspiracy*, William Heinemann Ltd, London, 1988.

Craik, Jennifer, *The face of fashion: cultural studies in fashion*, Routledge, London and New York,1993.

Cunningham, Patrick A. & Lab, Susan Voso (eds), *Dress and popular culture*, Bowling Green University Popular Press, Ohio, 1991.

De Pietri, Stephen & Leventon, Melissa, *New look to now: French haute couture, 1947–1987*, Fine Arts Museum of San Francisco, Rizzoli, New York, 1989.

De Teliga, Jane, *Project 33 Art Clothes*, Art Gallery of New South Wales, Sydney, 1980 (exhibition room brochure).

Farren, Mick, *The black leather jacket* Plexus Publishing Ltd, London, 1985.

'Fashion: little earth', *The Face*, no. 89, February 1996.

Franklin, Caryn, 'Rule Britannia', interview with Vivienne Westwood, *i-D*, The Metropolitan issue, no. 45, London, 1987.

Gaines, Jane & Herzog, Charlotte (eds), *Fabrications: costume and the female body*, Routledge, London, 1990.

Grauman, Brigid, 'Dirk Bikkembergs', *The Face*, no. 99, July/August, 1988, pp. 70–5.

Hebdige, Dick, *Subculture the meaning of style*, Methuen & Co, New York, 1979.

Holborn, Mark, *Issey Miyake*, Tascher, Germany, 1995.

Howell, Georgina, *In vogue*, Condé Nast Publications, New York, 1976.

Issey Miyake: Ten Sen Men, The 1st Hiroshima prize, Hiroshima City Museum of Contemporary Art, Hiroshima, 1990.

Jones, Kayt, 'The Outsiders', *i-D*, The High Spirits issue, no. 78, March 1990.

Kennedy, Shirley, *Pucci, a renaissance in fashion*, Abbeville Press, New York, 1991.

Khornak, Lucille, *Fashion 2001*, Viking Press, New York, 1982.

Living Yesterday, Tomorrow, 1996 Australian lecture tour programme.

Lobenthal, Joel, *Radical rags: fashions of the sixties*, Abbeville Press, New York, 1990.

Lynam, Ruth (ed.), *Couture*, Doubleday & Company Inc., New York, 1972.

McDermott, Catherine, *Street style*, The Design Council, London, 1987.

McDermott, Catherine, *Essential design*, Bloomsbury, London, 1992.

McDowell, Colin, *McDowell's directory of twentieth century fashion*, Mulder, London, 1984.

McDowell, Colin, *The designer scam*, Hutchinson, London, 1994.

McDowell, Colin, *Dressed to kill*, Hutchinson, London, 1992.

McPhee, John & McCormack, Susan, *Urban tribalwear and beyond Peter Tully*, Australian National Gallery, Canberra, 1991 (exhibition room brochure).

Malossi, Giannino (ed.), *The sala bianca: the birth of Italian fashion*, Electa, Milan, 1992.

Martin, Richard & Koda, Harold, *Flair*, Fashion Institute of Technology, Rizzoli, New York, 1992.

Martin, Richard & Koda, Harold, *Infra — Apparel*, Metropolitan Museum of Art, New York, 1993.

Martin, Richard & Koda, Harold, *The historical mode: fashion and art in the 1980s*, Electa, Milan, 1992.

Melly, George, *Revolt into style*, Cox & Wyman Ltd, London, 1970.

Miyake, Issey, *Issey Miyake bodyworks*, Shogakukan, Tokyo, 1983.

Mower, Sarah, 'Gaultier', *Arena*, Summer (July/August) 1987, pp. 62–5.

Mulassano, Adriana, *The who's who of Italian fashion*, Edizioni G. Spinelli, Florence, 1979.

Piccolo, Steve (ed.), *The world of Missoni*, Electa, Milan, 1995.

Polhemus, Ted, *Streetstyle*, Thames & Hudson, London, 1994.

Polhemus, Ted, *Bodystyles*, Leonard Publishing, London, 1988.

Redhead, Steve, *The end-of-the-century party*, Manchester University Press, New York, 1990.

Rhodes, Zandra & Knight, Anne, *The art of Zandra Rhodes*, Jonathon Cape, London, 1984.

Robbie, Angela, *Zoot suits and second-hand dresses*, MacMillan, London, 1989.

Yves Saint Laurent, Metropolitan Museum of Art, Thames & Hudson, London, 1984.

Yves Saint Laurent images of design 1958–1988, Alfred A. Knopf, New York, 1988.

Yves Saint Laurent Retrospective, Art Gallery of New South Wales, Beaver Press, Sydney, 1987.

Silverman, Debra, *Selling culture: Nancy Reagan, Diana Vreeland, Bloomingdale's and the Met*, Pantheon Books, New York, 1986.

Sischy, Ingrid & Celant, Germano, 'Editorial', *Art forum*, New York, 1982, p. 35.

Steele, Valerie, *Women of fashion: twentieth century designers*, Rizzoli, New York, 1991.

Tapert, Annette, 'For collectors: Beverley Birks', *Architectural Digest*, October, 1994, pp. 30–40.

Warhol, Andy & Hackett, Pat, *Popism*, Hutchinson, London, 1981.

Westwood, Vivienne, 'Royal flush', *i-D*, The Holiday issue, No. 50, London, 1987, pp. 55–6

White, Edmund, 'The last emperor', *The Australian Magazine*, 19–20 November 1994, pp. 20–6.

Wilson, Elizabeth, *Adorned in dreams: fashion and modernity*, Virago, London, 1985.

Quant, Mary, *Quant by Quant*, Redwood Press, London, 1966.